STILL IMAGES

IN

MULTIMEDIA

Mikkel Aaland

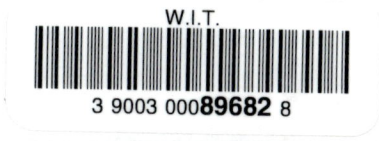

Hayden Books

Publisher
  Lyn Blake

Publishing Manager
  Laurie Petrycki

Managing Editor
  Lisa Wilson

Marketing Manager
  Nancy Price

Acquisitions Editor
  Robin Graham

Development/Copy Editor
  Beverly Scherf

Technical Editor
  Maria Yap

Publishing Coordinator
  Rosemary Lewis

Cover Designer
  Karen Ruggles

Book Designer
  Sandra Schroeder

Manufacturing Coordinator
  Brook Farling

Production Team Supervisor
  Laurie Casey

Production Team
  Daniel Caparo
  Terrie Deemer
  Krena Lanham
  Joe Millay
  Christine Tyner
  Pamela Volk
  Karen Walsh

Indexer
  Erika Millen

Still Images in Multimedia
©1996 Mikkel Aaland

Library of Congress Catalog Number: 96-75188
ISBN: 1-56830-273-8

Copyright © 1996 Hayden Books

Printed in the United States of America
1 2 3 4 5 6 7 8 9 0

This book was produced digitally by Macmillan Computer Publishing and manufactured by Shepard Poorman Communications Corporation, Indianapolis, Indiana.

Warning and Disclaimer

About the Author

Mikkel Aaland is a professional photographer, author, and co-founder of Tor Productions, a multimedia company specializing in the use of the still image in the new media. A contributing photographer for *Wired* magazine, he also has written for *Digital Creativity*, *Pre*, *MacWeek*, and *Graphis*.

Trademark Acknowledgments

Dedication

To Guillaume, who loves movies and multimedia.

Acknowledgments

Along the digital path many people offered me words of advice, wisdom, and encouragement—many of whom I acknowledged in my last book, *Digital Photography*. For this book, I would specifically like to thank: Marsha Weiner, Bernard Ohanian, Martha Avery, Cathy Fowler, Sarah Lazin, Rudy Burger, Anne Russell, Maggie Hallahan, Lori Barra, Blase Tobias and Dave Harrod at Drexel University (where I was reminded that content matters more than technology), Scott Sedlik, Mark Daniel, Kristy Heilman, Tom Wear, Doug Rowan, Christopher Pesce, Lisa Anderson, and Curtis Wong at Corbis who very generously gave me their time and attention, Matt Herron, Katherine Pfaff, Dave Drum, Dave Macias, Adriann Ligtenberg and Bill Krause of Storm Technologies, Paul McDougall, Michael O'Conner, Sonya Schaefer, Bob Stein, Cynthia Carris, Mac McCall, Eric Kotila, Robb Lazarus, George Arabian, and Rick Dalmazzi of DCI, Chris Vail, Tom Mogensen, Alexis Gerard, Paul Saffo, Rick Smolan, John Plunkett, Jacques Gauchey, Paul Foldes, Andrew Eisner, James Cowlin, Dave Pola, Jack Jackson and Julie Turkovitz of Scitek, Monica Suder, John Schultz, Steve Guttman, Tripp Mikich, Scott Highton, Ted Evans, Cathy Clarke of DXM, and Robin

Graham, Lisa Wilson, and Sandra Schroeder of Hayden Books who brought everything together.

I especially want to thank Michael Rogers for his insightful foreword and continuing friendship; the creative folks at Option X (Sean Parker, Maria Yap, Susan DuSchane, Laura Latham,and Jenny McMahon) who carefully reviewed the manuscript, offered plenty of useful comments and, at the last minute, provided some Photoshop expertise; Michael Nolan, for his vision to acquire and publish this book; Beverly Scherf, my development editor at Hayden, who was both supportive and a pleasure to work with; Pamela Signori for transcribing tapes and helping research and organize the appendix material; Nathan Benn and Rebecca Abrams for their open arms; and finally, and most importantly, my wife Rebecca, who carried the full weight of one of our other projects, and made time to help me with this one.

Hayden Books

The staff of Hayden Books is committed to bringing you the best computer books. What our readers think of Hayden is important to our ability to serve our customers. If you have any comments, no matter how great or how small, we'd appreciate your taking the time to send us a note.

You can reach Hayden Books at the following:

Hayden Books

201 West 103rd Street

Indianapolis, IN 46290

Email addresses:

America Online: Hayden Bks

Internet: hayden@hayden.com

Visit the Hayden Books Web site at http://www.hayden.com

Contents at a Glance

Table of Contents

Foreword

I've spent 20 years in print media, telling stories on paper with words and photographs, so sometimes my colleagues look askance at my immersion in projects such as Newsweek's CD-ROM and online ventures. Is this yet another challenge to the dominance that the word and still image once held on the imagination of the world? I assure my coworkers that our efforts aren't likely to make anyone of my generation obsolete; with luck, maybe someday new media will help pay our pensions.

But the real reason for my interest in the new technology is much deeper: I believe that multimedia, far from undercutting text and the still image, is the best thing to come along for both since the advent of television. Multimedia, in fact, can do much to restore the value of the word and still image in a world temporarily overwhelmed by passive video.

I say temporarily because television as it exists today is an unfinished medium. Indeed, a few generations from now, kids will wonder why we put up with our broken boxes for so many decades before we thought to repair them. Now, with the dawn of interactive multimedia, the television repair job has begun—text and the still image can achieve parity with video—and books like *Still Images in Multimedia* are both the inspiration and instruction for the work that needs to be done.

The simple flaw in conventional "passive" television is that it allows the user no control over timing, which renders it inherently hostile to print and still images. Both are forms that require individual time to regard. No person reads, comprehends, or enjoys text and images at precisely the same rate as any other.

That's why, on television, when one wants to present text, scrolling is unsatisfactory (since reading rates differ) and directors are left with what I call the "PBS method," where the star astronomer or philosopher walks across an open field and recites her lines while an elaborate tracking shot tries to keep it all looking lively. These days, whenever I see an awkwardly strolling narrator reciting a lengthy paragraph, I long for a "text" button on my television remote control.

Similar constraints exist for still images in passive video. Every once in a great while, someone lets a Ken Burns do a video documentary primarily composed of stills, but it's a risky gamble for television, where lingering over an image a moment too long can result in wholesale zapping by an impatient audience. In a cruel irony, however, even as television's lockstep timing provided no new venue for classic photojournalism, the sudden proliferation of video imagery in the Fifties hastened the death or downsizing of many existing media outlets for the still image.

And so, in the early 90s, when video first became widely available for CD-ROM-based multimedia, developers raised on television imagery were at first disappointed that for storage reasons they could use only relatively short pieces of video in their early productions. Some turned to multiple still images as "surrogate video"—and now we're coming to understand that sequenced stills, far from a video substitute, are a powerful story-telling technique on their own. In addition, for the new multimedia audience, 15 seconds of passive video often feels like the rest of their life. As information consumers newly in control of our electronic media, we don't want to be forced to watch anything we haven't chosen to watch—and if we're interested, we want it to stay on the screen until we're done.

Curiously, passive television is itself trying to overcome its fundamental flaw with stylistic devices. Consider MTV-style video editing, which is now so quick-cut that it often becomes, de facto, rapidly sequenced stills. But those "surrogate stills" aren't under viewer control—and there's a fundamental difference between composing a sequence of stills grabbed from video and building one of true still images. One might think of a video clip, composed for motion, as a single word—take one frame out of it and it's often only as powerful as a single letter. On the other hand, a stream of still images is more like a sentence—a single frame maintains the meaning and resonance of a complete word.

In short, new media—CD-ROM, the Internet, interactive television, or however we finally learn to deliver our bits—offers the opportunity for a remarkable renaissance in the art and appreciation of the still image. We mustn't let the moment slip away. It will grow ever easier to incorporate full-motion video into interactive communications, and as that happens, the still image needs to have firmly established its place and importance in the grammar of the medium.

That's a tall task in an electronic medium that—by virtue of engineering—seems so suited to video and so removed from paper. But I've worked with few people more capable of the challenge than Mikkel Aaland. He combines a firm understanding of what can be done today with a keen vision of what will be done tomorrow, informed by a deep regard, both artistic and technical, for the roots of the still image. *Still Images in Multimedia* clearly sets forth both the techniques and the opportunities; the future of the medium is up to us.

Michael Rogers

Vice President, Post-Newsweek New Media

Managing Editor, Newsweek InterActive

na007117.JPG   DL001946.JPG   a1028256.JPG   ih000566.JPG

sc002278.JPG   ih109313.JPG   a1012983.JPG   IH017808.JPG

th002198.JPG   ih023053.JPG   IH024436.JPG   th002202.JPG

ih015249.JPG   ih000552.JPG   ih106585.JPG   ih106651.JPG

ih106860.JPG   ih107000.JPG   ih109263.JPG   rt006102.JPG

Introduction

Multimedia has become a major industry, both pervasive and ever-growing. The still image, be it a photograph, painting, or drawing is a vital component of every multimedia project, whether it's a mass market CD-ROM title, a World Wide Web site, or a presentation to a live audience. Still images are easier and usually less expensive to use than full-motion video and equally as compelling. Witness, for example, Ken Burns' phenomenally successful Civil War series for PBS, or Corbis Media's best-selling CD-ROM "Passion for Art" and the other still image-based CD-ROM titles profiled in this book. Best of all, anyone with a basic desktop computer system can easily create inspirational, educational, or entertaining works by integrating still images— either alone, or as part of a sequence—with text and audio.

This book will show you, step-by-step, how to use still images in multimedia productions and on the Web. In Part 1, you'll learn how to find, create, and select the images you need. Part 2 will explain how to digitize and prepare the images. Part 3 will show you how to use the images by explaining basic design principles and giving you step-by-step examples. In the appendix, you'll find a list of content providers, tool makers, and other helpful resources. The accompanying CD-ROM is filled with images, sounds, and software tools to get you started. The CD-ROM also contains actual working examples of creative uses of still images in multimedia.

Throughout the book are useful tips tailored to a variety of budgets and project scales, because the needs of someone producing a commercial CD-ROM or a full-scale Web site are obviously different than those of someone putting together a project meant only for presentation to a small audience. You'll also find interviews with some of the world's most accomplished multimedia and Web producers and designers, who have generously volunteered to share their years of experience and wisdom.

Although you'll notice that certain popular and widely available software/hardware products are often cited—Adobe's Photoshop, Macromedia's Director, Equilibrium's DeBabelizer, and Kodak's Photo CD, to name a few—this book is by no means intended to be product or platform specific. Instead, whenever possible, the emphasis is on basic and advanced techniques that can be applied to a wide range of commercial software.

What It Takes to Get Started

This book assumes that you have a basic knowledge of how to use a personal computer, and own—or have access to—one of the hardware/software combinations listed below, or a very similar configuration. In some sections, the book also assumes a basic working knowledge of Adobe Photoshop and Macromedia Director, two of the most common multimedia software tools.

These sample hardware/software configurations are meant to be used for quick reference only. You'll find more details about specific software and hardware products in the relevant sections of the book, as well as manufacturers' addresses in the appendix. The accompanying CD-ROM contains trial versions of many popular software products.

As far as computer platforms go, we assume that most readers are using a Macintosh or a PC running a version of Microsoft Windows. Happily, for the readers who might be using other systems—such as a Unix-based system—much of the contents of this book still will be applicable not only because software is increasingly becoming multiplatform, but also because this book contains so much relevant material on production and design.

The following are some hardware/software combinations to consider:

Basic (under $1,000)

▶ Input device—None. Use Kodak's Photo CD process or a service bureau's instead.

▶ CPU—Macintosh with at least a 030 chip and 8 MB RAM. A PC with at least a 386 chip and 8 MB RAM.

▶ Monitor—A 13" monitor that can display 256 shades of gray or color.

▶ Storage device—At least a 40 MB hard drive and floppy disk capabilities.

▶ Software—Kodak Photo CD, MetaTool's QuickShow or shareware.

Good (around $3,500)

▶ Input device—Add to above: A 24-bit flatbed scanner for flat art or a video digitizer.

▶ CPU—Macintosh with a 040 chip and 16 MB RAM. PC with a 486 chip, 16 MB RAM, and a sound card.

▶ Monitor—A 17" monitor and graphics card capable of displaying thousands of colors.

▶ Storage device—1 GB hard drive, a CD-ROM player, and an external removable drive.

▶ Software—Adobe Photoshop, Macromedia Director, and Adobe Persuasion.

Best ($10,000 and up)

▶ Input device—Add to above: A slide scanner or a 30-bit flatbed scanner capable of digitizing flat art as well as slides and negatives.

▶ CPU—A Power PC with 32 MB RAM. A Pentium-based PC with 32 MB RAM.

▶ Monitor—A 21" color monitor with a 24-bit graphics card.

▶ Storage device—Add to above: A CD-ROM writer.

▶ Software—Photoshop, Director, DCI ImageAXS, Adobe Premiere, Adobe Illustrator (or Macromedia Freehand), Fractal Painter, and Equilibrium DeBabelizer.

Presentation and Distribution

Here are some samples and very general possibilities for ways to show and distribute your work. Keep in mind that one of the most exciting and economical ways of showing your work is to put it on the World Wide Web, a topic that will be discussed in much more detail later.

Basic (under $50)

▶ Using a service bureau, create a one-of-a-kind Kodak Photo CD, or a CD-ROM.

▶ Copy your work onto floppy disks.

▶ Place your work on the Web.

Good (under $300)

▶ Convert your work onto a standard VHS tape using a computer/TV interface and distribute and show it using any consumer VCR and TV.

▶ Use a computer/TV interface to show your work in real-time on any TV monitor or video projector.

▶ Place your work on the Web.

Best ($2,000 on up)

▶ Show your work using your own LCD panel and an overhead projector.

▶ Purchase and use an LCD or video projector.

▶ Publish and distribute a fully developed CD-ROM title.

▶ Place your work on the Web.

All you need to do now is add your imagination, your skills, and of course, your still images!

IH027005.JPG IH027030.JPG IH027047.JPG IH027135.JPG

IH027169.JPG IH027216.JPG IH027358.JPG IH027378.JPG

IH027489.JPG IH027521.JPG IH027539.JPG IH027585.JPG

IH027605.JPG IH027642.JPG IH027649.JPG IH027748.JPG

IH027843.JPG IH027900.JPG ih137641.JPG

Before You Begin: Communication, Schedules, and Budgets

Knowing where you're going with your project is critical. It will influence the type of images that you ultimately decide to use, determine how much image preparation applies, and inspire the overall look and feel of the project. If you're vague about your goal, everything you do, from choosing the right image to the final design of your project, will be difficult. You'll find yourself constantly making subjective decisions without focus or clear intent, and the odds are good that your final piece will not command attention.

Communication 101

Answering the following three questions will help you define your goal:

- ▶ What are you trying to communicate?

- ▶ Who is your audience?

- ▶ What do you want as a result?

When you ask yourself the first question, also ask yourself: Am I communicating information about a particular product, or am I trying to convey a general idea or concept? Am I trying to communicate raw reference information, or am I trying to entertain?

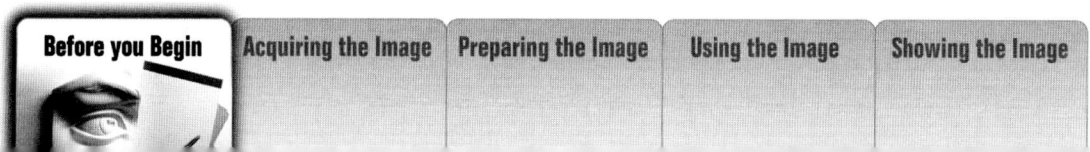

Recently, for example, I collaborated with a Virginia-based design group, Option X, on a Web site that showcased the digital art of the famous French multimedia artist, Chris Maker. We weren't selling anything. We weren't trying to communicate facts or figures. We were simply exposing the work of this great man to a world-wide audience. We kept this in mind during every step of the process, from the selection of content, to design, to the actual Web programming. As a result, the site is a bit chaotic and obscure but beautiful—just like Marker's work.

When determining who your audience is, remember that the closer you can identify a specific group, the easier it will be to tailor your message and create an appealing work. Professional market researchers often create profiles of audiences by taking into consideration such things as gender, age, education, values, tastes, demographics, and income.

Personally, I find it best to visualize a small group (7–10) of friends, relatives, or colleagues that I want to see my work. I write their names on a piece of paper and create a profile of each person. Much like a professional researcher might do, I ask myself: What do these people actually need? How can my work help them achieve this need? What is the best way of providing this information to them?

Finally, ask yourself what you want as a result of your efforts. Are you selling a product? Then sales is likely your desired outcome. Are you trying to make your company a better place to work? Then your message is one of inspiration and good will. Sometimes—like the time I created an electronic wedding photo album for a friend—I just wanted a smile or a laugh for my effort. Tangible or intangible, all goals are valid. But be clear about what you want in return for your efforts. Your clarity will help you create a more effective work and establish realistic expectations.

One of the most common mistakes people make is trying to say too much to too many people. The solution to this, which you've likely heard before, is keep it simple! You will be doing everyone a service.

Schedules and Deadlines

After you've identified your goal, you need a schedule to move you forward, step-by-step. In the digital world, schedules and deadlines are especially important. Anyone who has spent time working on an image with

Photoshop or creating an image with Fractal Design Painter knows there are limitless possibilities for refinement. A picture can always be a little better, a painting more realistic. A deadline becomes a boundary, a way to say "Enough!" To be realistic, schedules need to consist of a series of bite-sized deadlines, thoughtfully and realistically paced, so when the final deadline arrives most, if not all, of the work is already done.

The following table shows the major steps in a multimedia project with a rough estimate of the time that might be needed to finish three types of projects based on complexity.

	Simple	Moderately Complex	Complex
Planning and scheduling	1 day	2 days	3+ days
Brain storming/ creating the story	1–2 days	2–4 days	4+ days
Acquiring images and content	1–7 days	2–14 days	14+ days
Creating original images and content	1–7 days	2–14 days	14+ days
Processing the images	1–5 days	2–10 days	10+ days
Design and programming	2 days	4 days	15+ days
Testing	1/2 day	3 days	5+ days

Simple—A project that is created by one or two people using self-generated images, content, and already-owned software and hardware.

Moderately complex—A project that requires some outside content, services, and outside creative talent such as designers, illustrators, or photographers.

Complex—A full-blown multimedia project that requires retaining producers, lawyers, art directors, programmers, and marketing people.

The better you plan and schedule your project, the more you'll save time and money.

Here are some commonly underestimated or forgotten considerations that can impact a schedule:

- ▶ The time it takes to learn new software or to operate unfamiliar equipment

- ▶ Technical problems

- ▶ Rewrites

- ▶ The time it takes to obtain permissions and clearances for the use of outside content

- ▶ The time it takes to actually receive funding

- ▶ The additional time that is needed with a project that involves collaboration or sign-offs from higher-ups

- ▶ Vacations and holidays

- ▶ Illness

Keep in mind that even with the most realistic schedule, things go wrong. I was working on a half-million dollar CD-ROM project that was right on schedule, until one of the key software programmers unexpectedly left. Finding a replacement and getting him up to speed put the project way behind schedule. Ultimately, we missed an important shipping deadline because no contingency for the programmer's departure had been planned.

Budgets

Budgets are another real-world restraint that help define and shape a project. Regardless of who is financing the project, you or someone else, there is a finite amount of money that you can apply to your project. It must be wisely allocated.

How much you spend, and where you spend it, will be largely dependent upon the scope of your project and what you expect in return. It also will depend on what resources you have available, such as hardware/software.

Most important, the budget will depend on the content. I've seen compelling multimedia projects created by individuals for a few hundred dollars, who generated their own content and used borrowed equipment. I've also been involved with projects that cost hundreds of thousands of dollars and required consultants, freelance designers, and editors—and nearly all the content was bought from outside sources.

Here are some of the key budget categories that must be considered when creating a multimedia project based on still images:

▶ Content (including still images, text, reference material, and sound)

▶ Outside help (including programming, production, design, writing, research, editing, and proofreading)

▶ Legal fees

▶ Clearances

▶ Distribution (including WWW server costs, CD-ROM burning, floppy disks, and so on)

▶ Overhead (including computer hardware/software, telephone, and other incidentals)

Here are some tried-and-true ways of saving money:

▶ Generate your own content.

▶ Use and choose outside help carefully.

▶ Avoid rush charge expenses by scheduling more time.

▶ Talk with others who have done a similar project. Buy them lunch. Promise them credit. They've been in the trenches and have learned where to find the cheapest way to digitize an image, who is the best designer, and ways to get around software/hardware limitations.

Presenting Your Work

Early on, and preferably right now, you should make a decision about how your work will be distributed and seen. Every delivery method—be it a video projector, a CD-ROM, the WWW, or a floppy disk—has unique production requirements. Creating for the Web, for example, means taking into consideration low bandwidth and incompatible browsers, and using special compression techniques. You will therefore process and use images meant for the Web differently than, say, if you were creating a CD-ROM.

Case Study:
Robb Lazarus, DCI

Lazarus comes to multimedia from a background in psychology, technology, and business. At Digital Collections International (DCI) he puts all three disciplines to good use. Lazarus is DCI's project manager in charge of CD-ROM title production and creating imagebases for commercial and institutional purposes.

DCI was founded in 1989 by Dr. Stuart Marson. Like many high tech companies, DCI is not easily defined. Both a tool maker and content publisher, they create image management software such as ImageAXS. They have staked out the high end of CD-ROM publishing, and have focused on producing titles with scholarly and artistic merit that appeal to a sophisticated audience. Some of their titles to date include: "Great Paintings of the Frick Collection," "Masterworks of Japanese Painting," "Ancient Egyptian Art from the Brooklyn Museum," "1,000 Years of Russian Art," and their immensely popular CD-ROM featuring the work of the photographer Robert Mapplethorpe.

Lazarus:

Be prepared to spend a lot of time and be prepared to experiment. Allot plenty of time to trying different ways of doing things and looking at the results. If you can remove some of the time pressures, you can turn something that might otherwise be enormously frustrating into something that is more fun and experimental. If there is a constant time pressure, dead ends and blind alleys will become constant sources of stress. Also, always start out with the best equipment possible. It won't be the best in six months, but start out with it anyway.

Part I

Acquiring the Image

ih108270.JPG   na007115.JPG   RW005849.JPG   NA002967.JPG

IH014405.JPG   AL012109.JPG   DL001728.JPG   I1001403.JPG

ma13414a.JPG   IH019454.JPG   I1001383.JPG   th001127.JPG

AL004561.JPG   na007895.JPG   IH024090.JPG   ih000211.JPG

na007117.JPG   DL001946.JPG   a1028256.JPG   ih000566.JPG

Chapter 1

Finding the Images

Most multimedia projects require two classes of still images: those that already exist and those that don't. Existing images need to be found, and those that don't exist need to be created. In this chapter you'll discover how to find the right image among the millions that already exist. Creating your own—or hiring someone to create it for you—is discussed in the next chapter.

The most commonly used sources of still images are any of the hundreds of commercial image providers located around the country. These agencies—such as Corbis, Picture Network International (PNI), Comstock, Image Bank, and MP©A, to name a few—make it their business to find and sell the image you need. Some, like Corbis, PNI, and Comstock, are large companies with hundreds of thousands of general interest images. Other agencies are smaller and may carry only specialized subjects, such as animals or wooden boats or news photographs. MP©A (Media Photographers Copyright Association) is unique in that it is owned and operated by a collective of some of the world's most renowned photographers. In addition to these commercial providers, still images can be found all over the world in private, corporate, and public collections and institutions. (A listing of image providers is included in the appendix). Still images exist in a variety of forms including prints, negatives, slides, or half-toned reproductions. More and more still images are being stored digitally.

Browsing through the plethora of images and finding the right ones for your project can be both tedious and rewarding. This process often requires using a combination of high-tech tools and old-fashioned "gumshoe" ingenuity. You actually can go to museums, libraries, government, and corporate offices and search by hand for the images you need. Or you can use a high-speed

modem to contact any of a number of commercial image providers who have digitized and carefully cataloged their collections of images. You also can purchase and browse CDs containing thousands of digital images usually organized by topic, such as landscapes or animals.

Depending on your circumstances, you might consider hiring a professional to conduct the search for you. These picture editors or picture researchers make it their job to help you estimate and manage picture budgets, find the right images, and select and edit the images for you. (Ways to contact these professionals are listed in the appendix.)

The Process

Whatever method you use, here are some things to keep in mind when searching for the right image for your multimedia or Web project.

- ▶ Know and be able to articulate your project clearly to a potential image provider. Believe it or not, money is not the only motivation for selling an image. Image providers have pride in their work and want to know that their images will be treated with respect. This is especially true when dealing with museums and institutions.

- ▶ Be prepared for technophobic types who don't have a clue what multimedia is. Sure they've heard of it, but they've never seen it and are likely to be defensive unless you are patient and carefully explain what you are doing.

- ▶ Create a list of the images you need, including descriptions. This list will come in handy when contacting possible sources.

- ▶ Give yourself plenty of time to negotiate the rights to the images you decide to use. This step invariably takes longer than you expect.

- ▶ Unless you absolutely have no choice, avoid dependence on one source or one image. This dependence weakens your ability to negotiate effectively and can put your project in a tenuous position.

- ▶ Keep a picture log. Include a description of the project, image sources used, the number of images from each source, when and from whom images were received, a log-in number, and any special handling instructions for individual images. Keep a record of all correspondence with your log.

▶ After you make a final selection of images, create a permission log. Carefully describe the image, the source, exactly what rights have been negotiated, any restrictions or special conditions, and, finally, what you paid for the image.

In regard to the image, consider the following things:

▶ Keep in mind the special limitations of the electronic medium. Most multimedia and Web projects are viewed on a monitor with an aspect ratio of 4:3 (computer) or 2:2.66 (NTSC television), a ratio that favors horizontal images over vertical ones. Remember that a common 35mm slide has a ratio of 2:3, so with full screen viewing some cropping will occur and you will lose the edges of the image. Keep the "action" in the center of the image and remember that because of the lower resolution of most monitors, complex images are not as dramatic or effective. Also, watch your colors. Television, for example, doesn't handle red or magenta well.

▶ Consider how your images will relate to each other. Look for obvious juxtapositions of shapes and forms and shadows. You can simulate movement by looking for images of the same subject taken moments apart that can be sequenced; for example, of someone walking or a flag waving.

▶ If text or graphics need to be added to an image, look for images with lots of open space.

▶ If a digital file is provided, make sure the resolution is sufficient for your purposes. Also, make sure the digital file is in a file format that is compatible with your system. (Typically, images are provided in TIFF, PICT, EPS, or JPEG formats.)

▶ If a digital file is provided, find out what, if any, image processing has been done. Image processing includes gamma and color correction, and dust and noise removal and can take a long time if you do it yourself.

You also should know the rules involved in using still images. Consider the following:

▶ Know the limitations required by the image provider. Some institutions, for example, will not allow any manipulation of their images. Journalistic or documentary images also are often restricted.

▶ Avoid working with original slides or prints. If you must work with them, return them as soon as you have created a digital file. It will cost you a great deal if you lose or damage original artwork, including negatives and slides.

▶ Make sure the image provider has the right to sell electronic rights. Many visual artists, who don't want their work sold in digital form for fear of losing control, have work that resides with commercial agencies. (A digital file, after all, can be infinitely duplicated with no loss of quality.)

▶ Make sure the image provider has model and property releases on file. (See Chapter 3 for more details about this and other legal issues.)

Purchasing Rights from a Commercial Provider

Most of the time, when you buy an image from a commercial provider, you are not buying the image or its underlining copyright. You are buying the right to use the image for a particular project. The provider retains the copyright. The scope of these rights is negotiable. Generally, the bigger your project, the wider its dissemination, and the longer duration of time that you want the rights, the more you'll pay.

Of course, a buyout of all rights is possible but usually only for a large sum of money. Buyouts assure the buyer that no one else will use the image, which may be important for specific uses, such as advertising. In general, however, buyouts are not necessary. Instead, a limited duration exclusivity can be negotiated.

What can you expect to pay for an image when you negotiate with a commercial image provider? It varies depending on specific criteria. When you call an image provider, it is a good idea to know the following to facilitate the negotiations:

▶ The number of CDs or other delivery systems and range (local, national, or international) of your production. Prices for images used on the Web usually are determined by the placement of the image (for example, home page or linked page), the size of the image, and the length of time you want to keep the image as part of your site. One-year licensing is typical.

▶ The scope of the rights you want to purchase (for example, one-time rights, first-time rights, or multiple-production rights).

▶ The type of production. Editorial and educational usage generally is less expensive than advertising or corporate usage.

▶ How will the image be used? Rights will be less expensive if the image is part of a fast-moving multimedia sequence, and more expensive if it is used as a large "key" image on a home page on the Web.

Having said all this, keep in mind that there are no "set" fees for stock images. Depending on the usage, they can cost as little as $10 or as much as several hundred dollars.

NOTE   Most providers charge a nominal "research" fee, which is often waived if you actually buy an image.

Image providers generally charge what the market will bear, although at this time "new media" is such a new business that a lot of confusion and uncertainty exists about what is a realistic and fair price to charge for digital images. It is important to remember that most providers are willing to negotiate, especially if you are buying more than one image.

Acquiring Images from Museums and Public Archives

Economical and often overlooked sources of images are museums, such as those found within the Smithsonian Institution, and public archives, such as the Library of Congress. Because many of the images are considered to be in the public domain, there are few if any reproduction restrictions and no fees to pay. (Often there is a nominal charge for copy prints or negatives).

NOTE   Nine million images, spanning the years of 1850-1985, are housed within the Library of Congress. These images are gifts from private individuals, corporations, and photographers.

Other institutional sources of photographs include the National Archives, the National Aeronautics and Space Administration (NASA), The National Museum of American History, The Metropolitan Museum of Art, The New York Public Library, and The British Museum. A more complete list of these museums and archives and a bibliography of source books is included in the appendix.

Although most institutions have offices devoted to providing imaging services, dealing with them is not the same as dealing with commercial image providers. Their primary mission is not commercial but educational. Prices—when they apply—may not be their number-one concern while other details are. It's common for a museum to prohibit a user from placing any text on top of an image, to crop an image, or to use the image in an exclusive manner. Museums always want to be credited, and there are often precise stipulations on how the credit is written and where it must appear.

Keep in mind that museums and other such institutions take a long time to process requests for images and reproduction rights. If the source is abroad, it will take even longer.

Online Access

Today many traditional image providers—and a whole slew of newcomers—have placed their collections online making it easier than ever to track down the images you need. All you have to do is use your computer, modem, telephone line or cable, an Internet access provider, and a browser to access the World Wide Web, where most of these services can be found.

These online providers range in size from individual visual artists who have Web sites and offer very specific sets of images to large companies, such as Corbis, PNI, or Comstock, and Image Bank, who offer thousands of images from around the world. Many of the museums and institutions mentioned already have placed a limited number of their collections online.

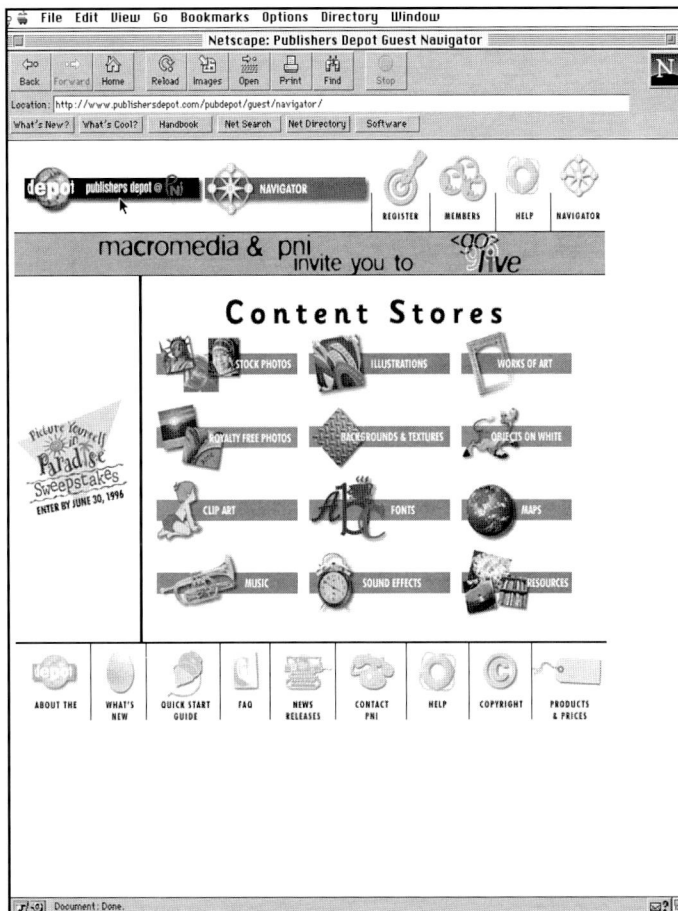

Figure 1.1   PNI's Web site, Publisher's Depot.

In theory, online access to images is a multimedia producer's dream. The entire process of searching, finding, and retrieving still images can be done in front of a computer terminal from anywhere in the world. Using a common 28.8K modem, a compressed, full-screen color image takes only a few minutes to download. (Speeds vary depending on the amount of compression, the speed of your computer, and the phone line quality.) Even price and rights can be negotiated online.

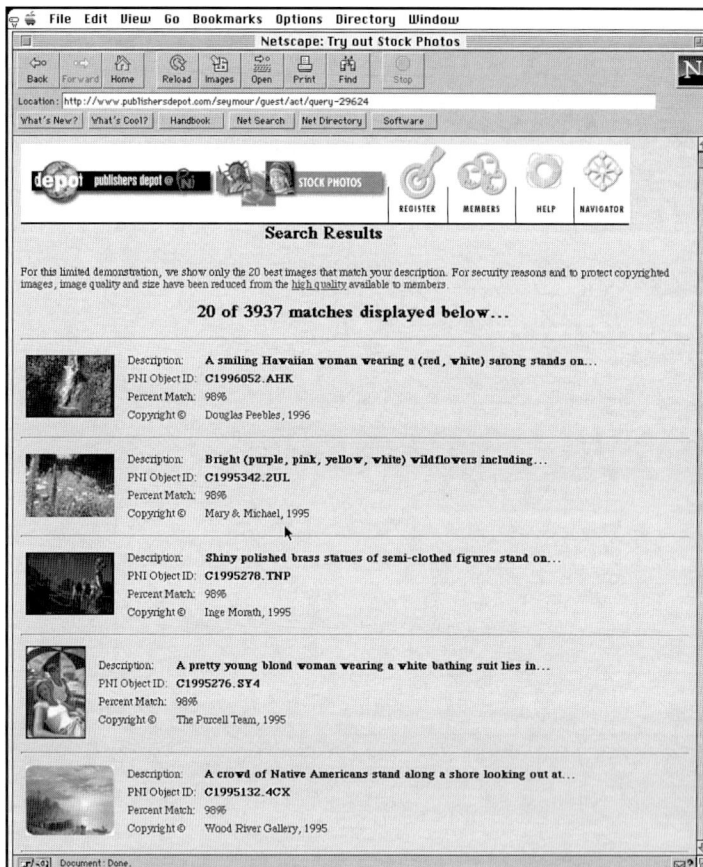

Figure 1.2 The results from a PNI online image search using the identifying word "beauty."

Online image access is a relatively new phenomena, and there are limitations. The time it takes to download dozens of screen resolution images adds up. Search and retrieval methods are often nonexistent, so finding the image you need can be like finding a needle in a haystack. Payment methods are not standardized. Some image providers accept credit cards, while others require you to fill out a credit application.

All of this will change very soon. ISDN (Integrated Services Digital Network) service, which employs new technologies and existing copper phone lines and is at least five times faster than the current fastest modem/telephone line capability, has come down in price and is now available in most metropolitan areas of the country. Cable modems, which are used with cable TV lines and are fast enough to send full-motion video in real time, are being test marketed all over the country. Two new technologies, SDSL (Symmetric Digital Subscriber Line) and ADSL (Asymmetric Digital Subscriber Line), may soon impact the market for high-speed transmission. Both systems work on regular copper phone lines and deliver data 10 to 50 times faster than ISDN. Search and retrieval software that uses "fuzzy" logic is being developed that will greatly speed up the process of finding the images you need. And finally, digital cash, which allows you to purchase things online with full security, is around the corner.

In the meantime:

▶ Use 28.8K modems. They cost $100-$200. See if ISDN is available in your area. (Because ISDN is all-digital transmission you don't need a modem. The necessary hardware is basically a switcher box that costs around $200-$300. Monthly service charges vary, but $20-$30 is typical. These prices are likely to keep dropping.) Cable modems may also be an option in your area. Watch for the introduction of SDSL and ADSL services.

▶ Find a local Internet provider. Many charge around $20 a month for nearly unlimited access to the Net.

▶ Experience the best of the Web by using the most recent version of a Web browser (Netscape or Microsoft's Explorer are the two most popular). Software features are added regularly.

▶ Don't hesitate to contact one of the larger online image providers to assist you, such as Corbis or PNI (listed in the appendix). It's in their interest to see that you get online and thereby have access to their services. They will gladly guide you through the necessary steps as well as inform you about Internet service providers in your area.

▶ Don't be discouraged if you don't find what you want online. Often image providers put only a very small portion of their holdings online. Call them and ask specifically for the types of images you are looking for. They will either create special electronic "light boxes" that you can later view online, or they will send you a CD with the image you requested.

Images are often sent as JPEG formatted files, with varying amounts of compression. Sometimes they are transferred in GIF format, but because GIF doesn't support 24-bit color its use is limited. Once you've downloaded the images, you can convert them to whatever format you want using Photoshop or DeBabelizer.

NOTE   Besides actually downloading an image file you can "capture" images from the screen by purchasing special software, such as CameraMan from Motion Works for the Macintosh and WinCapture from Professional Capture Systems for the PC. On most Macintos Computers, Command-Shift-3 will record everything on the screen as a PICT file. Some versions of Windows also have a built-in screen capture feature (Print Screen key) that will save the screen to the Clipboard where it can later be pasted into image processing software.

Images on a CD

Browse through any computer or graphic arts magazine and you will see advertisements for CD-ROM Clip Photos. One disc might advertise "100 Images of Angels of the Ages," or "100 Famous Beaches of the World," or "100 Images of the American Civil War." Many of the CDs contain specific items such as trees, flowers, undersea textures, or animals. There are no limits to what these CDs contain, and because the photographs are already in digital form, they are ready for near-instant placement in your production. (A list of companies that offer images on a disc is included in the appendix.)

CDs range in price from a few dollars to several hundred dollars, and often you get what you pay for. Many of the lower-priced CDs contain images of such poor quality that you'll end up using the CD as a coffee coaster. Some companies create inexpensive "sample" CDs that contain thumbnail resolutions so that you can actually get a good idea of the range of images before you buy the full resolution version. Many CDs contain images with inadequate resolution for printing that is perfectly acceptable for on-screen use.

To access images from these CDs you need a CD-ROM player connected to your computer. On most CDs individual images come in a variety of resolutions, mostly in TIFF format. Some CDs include image search software and electronic "lightboxes" for image editing. Licensing agreements vary. Some CDs are sold royalty free, which means you can use the images on the disc nearly any way you want for as long as you want. (The images, however, cannot be resold as individual images, nor can they be used in certain commercial applications without additional licensing.) Other CDs contain images that are meant only for personal viewing, and you must negotiate a separate license if you want to use the material commercially. Be sure to read the agreement provided with the CD to know exactly what your rights are. Because many of the CDs are mass-produced, you can't buy exclusive rights, and there is always the chance you will see the same image you choose in someone else's production.

Other Sources of Still Images

It's not a bad idea to be always on the lookout for still images. On the dusty shelves of a used bookstore or in the steel case files of a public relations agency, you might find images for a specific or potential project. You never know when a turn-of-the-century postcard, a movie still, or a collection of postage stamps might come in handy. It doesn't matter if the images aren't in digital form. In Chapter 4, you'll see how to convert them.

Keep in mind that just because you "found" the images in the public domain doesn't necessarily mean you have rights to use them. This is especially true if your project is of a commercial nature. (See Chapter 3 for more on legal details.) The following places might also be helpful in finding images:

▶ Newspapers and magazines provide a regular supply of still images. If you see an image you like, call the publication and ask how you can buy a copy.

▶ Family albums are treasure chests of still images. Whether it is your own or someone else's dusty album you found in an attic or garage sale, it is likely to be filled with photographs of historic cars, homes, and clothing styles.

► Flea markets and used bookstores are especially good for old postcards, old books, and other published material.

► Videos are repositories of millions of "frames" of individual images that can be "grabbed" and, with a little processing, made presentable as still images. (See Chapter 4 for more information.)

► Public relation firms have vast collections of commissioned images created to sell products or services. Often, rights and permissions are not an issue.

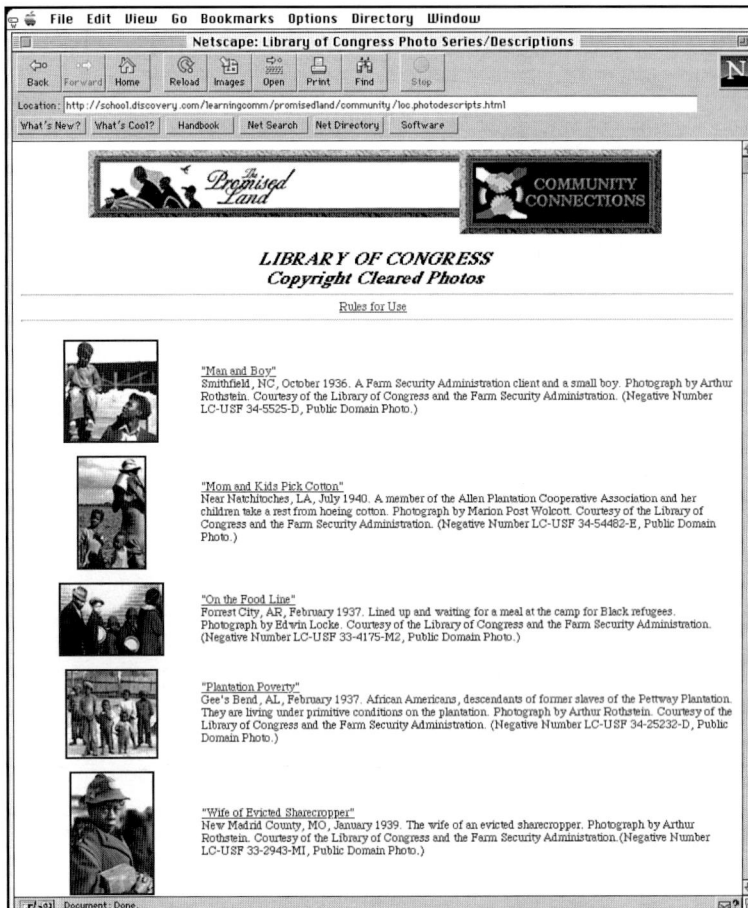

Figure 1.3 A screen shot from a Web site that provides public domain images.

Figure 1.4 A detailed view from the same site.

Case Study:
Bob Stein, Voyager

Bob Stein is the cofounder of Voyager, one of the earliest and most successful multimedia companies in the country. Founded in 1985, Voyager, which takes its name from the exploratory spacecraft, released laser discs of contemporary and classic films. In 1987, the company released its first HyperCard/computer-controlled interactive discs. In 1988, it released its first consumer CD-ROM, "Beethoven's Ninth Symphony." (Voyager can be contacted at www.voyagerco.com)

Stein:

Voyager's interest in still images is very closely related to our interest in text. What appeals to me about both text and still images is that they are media particularly suited for reflection. The most interactive thing that happens is a discussion between two people. And my favorite media are the ones that allow you to enter into a dialogue of a sort with an author. Because they happen at the producer's speed, most of the 20th century media—television, radio, movies— are very good at some things but they're not very good at actually letting you think along the way and question what you're seeing. They tend to be very moving and manipulative in the good sense of the word, but they don't really encourage the viewers to think about what they're looking at. In that sense, they're not as ideal for learning as still pictures and text.

A lot of times people will use Ken Burns [that is, the PBS Civil War Series] as an example of what you can do with still pictures. To me it's not a good example because he animates the pictures. Of course, when you look at a Ken Burns program it is a good example of the *value* of still pictures, and it shows what you can do with still pictures. It shows you can make still pictures into a movie very successfully. But to me, it subverts the principal value of the still picture, which is that the viewer has to be confronted. You've got to think about it. It doesn't do it for you, the way motion pictures do more easily.

The Pedro Meyer CD-ROM "I Photograph to Remember" [a moving story of the death of Meyer's father told with sequenced stills, voice-over, and music], which we published in the early 90s, sold very, very well, but I'm afraid that if it had come out today it might not have sold as well. Video is inexorably getting bigger and better, and I am afraid that it's going to marginalize still pictures. I think that's a terrible thing. But bad money drives out good money somehow, and this whole industry is moving toward an advertiser-supported mass market of one kind or another. Advertisers find it easier to sell Fritos with movies than they do with still pictures.

sc002278.JPG | ih109313.JPG | a1012983.JPG | IH017808.JPG
th002198.JPG | ih023053.JPG | IH024436.JPG | th002202.JPG
ih015249.JPG | ih000552.JPG | ih106585.JPG | ih106651.JPG
ih106860.JPG | ih107000.JPG | ih109263.JPG | rt006102.JPG
rt006099.JPG | IH023173.JPG | IH029786.JPG | IH029785.JPG

Chapter 2

Creating Your Own Images

There are many good reasons to shoot and create your own images. Shooting your own gives you aesthetic control and can save money. It also clarifies issues of copyright and ownership, which means that you can manipulate and crop the images any way you wish.

Modern tools combined with your creative vision simplify the process. In the past, many designers or project managers didn't think to pick up a camera themselves, but today's cameras, including digital models, make good picture-taking especially easy. Imaging, painting, and drawing software assist you to add special effects or to create collages from your original images or images that you have acquired from others.

Shooting your own will not be realistic in all circumstances, and you may want to hire a visual artist to create the image for you. How to find the right person and how to work together is discussed at the end of this chapter.

Cameras: Digital and Otherwise

Digital cameras are the perfect tool for creating still images to be used in multimedia. Rather than film, they store images on cards or on a computer storage device in a convenient digital form which can be immediately viewed on your computer screen. Digital cameras cost a little more than traditional cameras—from $500–$30,000—but by using a digital camera, you can actually save money in the long run. You never need to pay for film or processing, and since the photo is already in digital form, there is no need to use a scanner or to pay for digitizing the image. (See the Case Study at the end of this chapter.)

Before you Begin | **Acquiring the Image** | Preparing the Image | Using the Image | Showing the Image

Digital cameras range widely in quality and are manufactured by a variety of companies including Apple, Eastman Kodak, Sony, Fuji, and Nikon. Cameras with fixed lenses start at around $600 and produce pictures with enough resolution for the average screen presentation (640×480 pixels). Mid-range digital cameras use a traditional 35mm SLR camera body and cost anywhere from $10,000–$18,000. These cameras take interchangeable lenses, include motor drives, and create a digital picture with a resolution of 1280×1012 pixels or greater. The high-end digital cameras, which generally cost over $20,000, produce resolutions higher than 3072×2320 pixels. Unlike the low- and mid-range cameras mentioned above which are battery-powered and store the images onboard the camera, high-end digital cameras often require a tether to a computer and a 120V power supply. Because high-end cameras employ long exposures, they can be used only to take pictures of objects that don't move. (Because of their high resolution and great dynamic range they can be used instead of a flatbed scanner to scan oversized flat art.)

When using a digital camera, all the general rules of traditional photographic lighting, composition, and tone remain. Keep in mind, however, that because of the limited resolution of some of the digital cameras, you must shoot tight to avoid later cropping and enlarging the image, resulting in loss of image quality. Also, it's a good idea to test the camera for compatibility with your computer system to make sure the image quality is good enough for your purposes.

Although digital cameras have many qualities to recommend them, it's still a fact that traditional 35mm cameras and the Advanced Photo System (APS) recently introduced by major camera and film manufacturers have their own advantages. Cameras have evolved, just like the user-friendly computer you are likely working on. Auto focus, auto exposure, auto flash, even auto fill-flash are all part of the modern "intelligent" camera, available for reasonable prices ranging from $200–$500. Used in conjunction with a slide scanner or the Photo CD Process, traditional cameras give you the best of both worlds: an inexpensive, high-quality storage medium (a 35mm negative costs about 10 cents and represents about 20 million pixels or 60 MB of computer storage space) and the digital file required for multimedia applications. Keep the following in mind:

▶ SLR (Single Reflex Lens) cameras offer more control and features, but "point-and-shoot" cameras are often adequate for simple shots.

▶ A 35–90mm zoom lens will cover most of your needs.

- ▶ On-camera strobes should have the ability to be bounced off ceilings or bounce cards to soften and create flattering light.

- ▶ Shooting color slide film, such as Kodachrome or Fujichrome, will give you the best color fidelity and sharpness, but these films have little latitude and must be exposed carefully. Color print film, such as Extapress, Kodacolor, or Fujicolor, is much easier to use and is easily transferred to Kodak's Photo CD discs.

Shooting

The basic rules of shooting for multimedia are shoot a lot and shoot from different angles so that you can create sequences later. Multimedia projects generally use a lot of still images (there is no appreciable cost difference between using 10 images or 100), and film is relatively inexpensive. If you are using a digital camera, cost-per-frame is not a factor at all.

Here are some other things to keep in mind:

- ▶ People. When photographing people, the most important thing is to make the subject relax. This means *you* have to be confident and relaxed. Have a location in mind before the shoot. Be familiar with your equipment. Respect the subject's busy schedule and take as little time as possible. Wide-angle lenses will distort people's faces, so it's best to use a slightly telephoto lens (85–135mm). Indirect natural or strobe light, as from a window or a bounce flash, is flattering. Direct sunlight or strobes are not. As well as different angles, shoot people in various moods—a grimace here, a laugh there—and different poses—standing, sitting, or curled up.

- ▶ Places. A church or a tract home is deceptively difficult to shoot well. Avoid shooting at noon when light is contrasty. Sunlight is generally best in the morning and evening or when filtered through a layer of clouds. When the camera is pointed at an upward angle problems arise from converging lines that make a building look like a pyramid instead of a box. Special corrective lenses and cameras are available, but expensive. The problem can be avoided by keeping the camera and lens level to the ground and either moving far enough from the building or mounting a ladder to get the angle you need. Again, shoot different angles and perspectives. Shoot an overview as well as details. Always keep sequencing in mind.

▶ Things. Good lighting and composition can make inanimate objects come alive. Look for interesting angles and shoot them all. Experience with different backgrounds, both indoors and out. Play with light sources of different colors.

Finally, keep in mind that photography is a visual language dependent on light. It's often most effective when it speaks to the non-verbal, intuitive side of the brain, complementing words but not competing with them. A roadway sign on a lonely country road, for example, is not only shot because of its literal, verbal content, but also for its shape, the way that light strikes it, and the inherent tension between something man-made and something natural like the receding skyline. This visual language can be learned by taking classes and examining images in books and on CD-ROMs, seeing what works and what doesn't. It is also learned by going to exhibitions and art galleries; and finally, it is learned by looking around you, by paying attention to the way that winter light strikes a gnarled old oak tree or a young baby's face.

Manipulating Images

There is an infinite number of ways to manipulate a picture. Using software programs such as Photoshop, Painter, and Illustrator, it's a snap to add or remove elements from an image, add special effects such as motion blur, and to create collages and composites.

Image manipulation is the actual process of substantially altering an image from the original, sometimes subtle, sometimes gross, but always altering it from its original form. Keep in mind that image manipulation is not image processing, which generally consists of tonal correction, resizing, and removal of dust and noise.

NOTE   Image processing, which is a critical step in preparing still images for use in multimedia or on the Web, is discussed in Chapter 5.

It is particularly important that you make sure you have the rights to manipulate an image. Many images purchased from commercial image providers come with restrictions, and almost all images from institutions and museums come with specific requests not to alter them in any way.

A special note about documentary images: It is now easier than ever to blur the distinction between fact and fantasy. You can add a politician to an image of a presidential speech, or remove an unseemly power plant and replace it with a pristine bush. And yet every time an image is misrepresented, be it on a CD-ROM project or on the Web, an erosion of the power of the documentary image occurs.

When viewers see an editorial or documentary photo, they generally assume they are witnessing an attempt to objectively record an event in time and place. When viewers see an image presented in an illustrative or commercial context, they generally accept that this is an interpretive or artistic vision.

When images have been altered, avoid referring to images as photographs. Several professional photography organizations and agencies have wisely proposed the use of these words: photo montage, photo illustration, digital composites ("DC"), or digital enhancements ("DE") when images have been significantly altered. (The organizations agree that some image processing, such as color correction and contrast enhancement, is permissible provided that the fundamental content of the photograph is not changed.)

Common Manipulations

Here are a few examples of some of the more common image manipulations used in multimedia projects. For the examples in this book, I used Photoshop to do the following:

- ▶ Apply Motion Blur to an image

- ▶ Create a collage

- ▶ Add several elements to an image

Figure 2.1   Normal image.

Figure 2.2 Image with motion blur.

Figure 2.3   A collage: Step one.

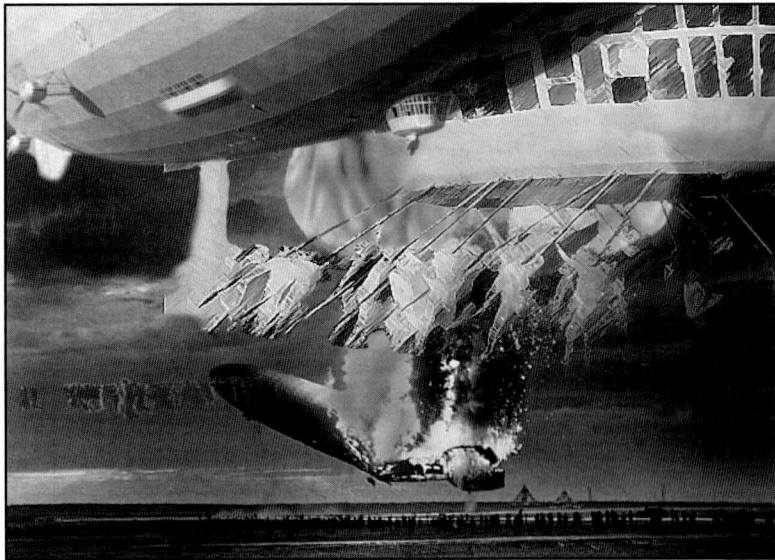

Figure 2.4   The finished collage.

Figure 2.5   The normal image.

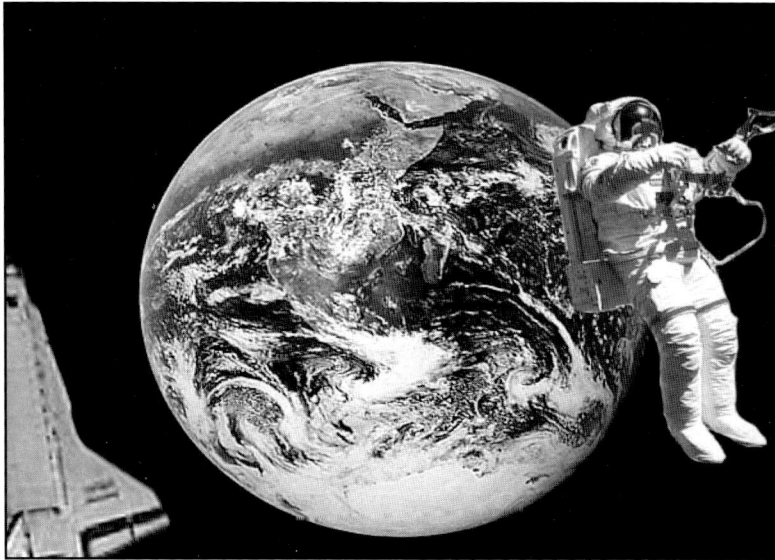

Figure 2.6   The image with added elements.

Hiring a Visual Artist

There are times when making your own image isn't practical, and finding the image you need in existing stock isn't possible. That's when you should consider hiring an imaging professional, or, as they are often called, a visual artist.

Photographers and illustrators are of particular value to a multimedia producer. These are professionals who make it their business to sell their skills on a freelance basis, hiring themselves out by the hour, day, or project. They are small businesses in the true sense of the word, often consisting of individuals working out of their home or a small office or studio, owning their own equipment and paying their own insurance and taxes. Increasingly, the distinction between photographers and illustrators is becoming blurred. More and more photographers are working with programs such as Photoshop to create photo illustrations. Illustrators are using photographs in their work. The computer is the common ground, changing the way people work and how they describe themselves.

Whether you hire a photographer, an illustrator, or someone who can do both will be dependent upon your particular project. Regardless, here are some things to keep in mind. When hiring someone, follow these considerations:

▶ Word of mouth is one of the best ways of finding a good visual artist. Another good way is to consult membership directories of professional organizations such as the American Society of Media Photographers (ASMP), Advertising Photographers of America (APA), Professional Photographers of America (PPA), and the American Institute of Graphic Artists (AIGA), (listed in the appendix). If you see an image in a magazine that you particularly like, check out the credit and call the magazine for the artist's phone number to directly solicit him or her.

▶ Set an appointment to see the artist's portfolio. The appointment also will give you a chance to feel the chemistry between you and the artist. Subjective things like this are often important. If a face-to-face meeting is not possible, see if the artist has images on a Web site you can view. Ask if the portfolio is available on a CD-ROM that you can see.

▶ Determine how long he or she has been in business. Being a professional means running a small business complete with a large overhead. Obviously, to be in business a long time takes both dedication and talent.

▶ Get references of the visual artist's other clients. It's not a bad idea to follow up on references.

▶ If the artist is a photographer, does he or she have a studio? This may be important if you are interested in complex product shots. Does he or she have experience traveling with lots of equipment? This is an important question if you are interested in shots that require out-of-town travel. Transporting camera and strobe equipment and dealing with the logistics of travel are acquired skills that not every photographer has.

▶ Determine the type of computer equipment the artist owns. Is it compatible with your system? Formats are often interchangeable, but not always.

When negotiating prices, consider that although many photographers and illustrators charge a variable day rate for their services, most are willing to consider half-day or even hourly rates. The type of job is considered. Most will not "work for hire," which means they retain the copyright and resale rights to the images they make. (Again, everything is negotiable, but be prepared to pay a lot more for work-for-hire contracts.) Remember that visual artists are always looking for good clients who will continue to hire them. If you fit this description, let them know because they will be more willing to offer special deals.

Expenses such as film processing and travel generally are paid by you. It's a good idea to get an approximate amount up front that a visual artist anticipates spending in expenses. Getting everything in writing can prevent misunderstandings.

Case Study:

The author on shooting digital stills for "Third Degree."

In the early '90s I was asked to justify the use of sequenced still images instead of full-motion video on a ground-breaking multimedia project, a CD-I game disc, loosely based on the popular board game Scruples. The script included 50 social dilemmas that the producers needed to establish visually. The producer had originally budgeted about $100,000 for a video crew and 37 days of shooting. I came back with a proposed budget of $30,000. This covered my day rate, my equipment and an assistant. Since I proposed shooting the entire job with an electronic still camera, there were no film and processing expenses.

The first thing I learned was to shoot a lot, since the production cost of using one photograph or twenty is nearly the same, and to shoot much less discriminately. Many times a producer found value in my outtakes, wanting a particular color or minute detail to include in a photo montage.

Since this was the first time I had put aside my traditional equipment and shot electronically, there was a myriad of unforeseen problems. For example, the early electronic cameras had a limited exposure latitude, which meant that correct exposure was critical, a problem that no longer exists with the newer digital cameras. We also quickly learned that there was no consistency between the playback unit, the camera monitor, and the computer monitor. In other words, there was no guarantee that what we were seeing on the monitor was actually what was being stored as a digital image in the computer. This problem was solved by employing an analog engineer who hooked up a wave-form monitor (a type of oscilloscope) and calibrated the playback unit, the video board, and the monitor.

I learned many lessons which continue to be relevant today. I learned to think in terms of sequenced images that actually build to a narrative. Although this process may sound a lot like film, the model that I looked toward was the comic strip which uses a few related frames to effectively tell a story. When I shot a door, I shot it open and closed. When I shot a curtain, I shot it in different positions. When I shot a car, I shot it in three or four different locations. When I shot an individual, I tried to capture his or her eyes both open and shut. This gave the producer a chance to build narrative sequences. I also kept in mind characteristics of the screen. Vertical images are more difficult to work with. I centered the action, and kept the images simple because of limited resolution (which remains a concern today).

When the entire job was complete, the show was shown to a select audience. Afterward, the audience was asked many questions. One of the questions concerned the still photographs: Did the use of still photos instead of full motion video bother you? No, they answered. Not one of the respondents even noticed still images had been used rather than full-motion video. For this test audience the important thing was understanding the narrative, which they did without difficulty.

IH029784.JPG   IH029783.JPG   IH029782.JPG   IH029781.JPG

ih029758.JPG   NA001382.JPG   mb015681.JPG   mb015676.JPG

mb015661.JPG   mb009211.JPG   mb009034.JPG   RW007079.JPG

RW007099.JPG   IH029927.JPG   IH029916.JPG   IH029932.JPG

NA005173.JPG   NA005113.JPG   NA005136.JPG   IH029980.JPG

copyright Corbis

Chapter 3

Special Considerations: Copyright, Releases, and Other Legal Issues

It's one thing to have the image or images you need, and quite another to possess the legal rights to use the image. Behind most images is a person, company, or institution who owns and controls the copyright to that image.

NOTE   This chapter is designed to make you aware of potential legal issues involved in using and distributing still images. It is not legal advice. If you have questions about the legal implications of a contemplated use, contact an attorney.

Even when the issue of copyright seems clear—for example, if you created the image yourself—it doesn't necessarily mean that you can use the image. Contained in many images are depictions of real and recognizable people, places, or things, all of which may have rights of privacy. An image may also depict underlying copyrighted art, which could require permission from the artist or the artist's estate before the image can be used.

Before you Begin   **Acquiring the Image**   Preparing the Image   Using the Image   Showing the Image

The consequences of not taking into consideration these legal questions of copyright and rights of privacy vary, depending on the type of project with which you are involved. Simply put, the more commercial your project is, or the more visible it is, the more careful you should be in seeing that all rights are taken into consideration. On the other hand, the legal system allows more leeway for educational and journalistic endeavors.

Copyright

Copyright law in the United States dates back to 1790 and was designed to protect the tangible *expression* of an idea (although not the idea itself) from unauthorized appropriation. This means that whenever an individual takes or makes a picture, he or she creates and owns what is known as intellectual property. Copyright ensures that the creator holds the right to copy, distribute, sell, or create derivatives of the original. These rights can be transferred to a second party, but only by the creator. The creator can then reclaim his or her rights after a period of time, if he or she so wishes.

Under the provision of the 1976 Federal Copyright Act, copyright automatically becomes the property of the creator from the moment of creation to 50 years beyond his or her life. The law applies to works created prior to January 1, 1978, except when the work was already in the public domain or copyrighted under the old law. (The old copyright act of 1909 stipulated that a copyright endured for 28 years and was renewable for another 28 years, plus one more extension of 19 years for a maximum of 75 years from publication.) When a copyright owner is a corporation, business, or employer, the protection lasts 75 years after publication or 100 years following creation, whichever is shorter. After that time the work goes into the public domain and may be reproduced by anyone without payment to the original copyright owner.

(Here is a good question: How does a museum that contains old paintings that are clearly beyond copyrightable age control their usage? They often do this by restricting photographic access to the images and periodically making their own photographs of the images, which are then copyrightable. In order to get a good photo of the image, you must go through the museum and use their photo, for which they charge a fee.)

What happens if you use a copyrighted image that is not yours and one that you didn't have permission to use? The law is clear and is summarized as follows:

▶ Profits from the sale of the work can be ordered transferred from you to the copyright owner

▶ Copies of the infringing work can be ordered destroyed

▶ An injunction against future infringement may be ordered against you

▶ You may be required to reimburse any financial loss occurred by the copyright owner

▶ Statutory damages can be assessed against you

▶ You can be ordered to pay all court costs and attorneys' fees

With this in mind, follow these guidelines:

▶ Don't take chances, especially if your project is of a commercial nature

▶ Purchase your images from a reputable stock house where you know that issues of copyright are clear (see below, "Rights of Privacy")

▶ Create your own content (see below, "Rights of Privacy")

▶ When in doubt, consult legal experts or use a professional copyright clearing service (see the appendix)

Rights of Privacy

Depending on your specific project and audience, there may be times when you need to obtain a special release for people, places, or things depicted in the images.

There is no straightforward logic or rule for determining when you need a release. For example, to use a picture of a celebrity who profits from his or her celebrity status requires permission from that celebrity or from his or her representative. On the other hand, the use of a picture of a politician, who is also a public figure, does not require a special release.

Obtaining clearances can take time, so it is a good idea to plan ahead. (In the appendix is a list of companies that specialize in obtaining clearances. If your project is of a commercial nature, the use of such a service is highly recommended.)

Editorial Usages

Clearances are not as critical when the image is used for editorial purposes. Editorial use involves using an image to portray or illustrate an event or issue that is currently newsworthy or of legitimate public interest. Keep in mind, however, that the boundaries between editorial and commercial/advertising can be crossed inadvertently. For example, if an image appears on the cover of a magazine, it is considered advertising and all the rules relating to advertising apply. Thus, model or property releases must be on file specifically releasing the right to use that image in a commercial manner. If the image depicts a minor, model releases are almost always required, even if the image is used editorially. Also, if an image of a private individual is used in a way that is libelous or ridicules or misrepresents that person, the depicted individual has the right to sue for compensation.

Advertising and Commercial

Releases for images that contain discernible people, places, or things are almost always needed when the image is destined for commercial or advertising purposes. Exceptions to this rule are images that are in the public domain. These are pictures whose copyright has expired or pictures that were taken on behalf of the United States government. By definition, these pictures are subject to appropriation by anyone, although some U.S. government pictures come with certain commercial restrictions.

Fair Use

Releases generally are not needed when the image is to be used in a way that has been defined as "fair use," which includes criticism, comment, news reporting, teaching (including multiple copies for classroom use), scholarship, or research. According to the courts, the factors to be considered in determining whether the use made of a work in any particular case is a fair use shall include:

▶ The purpose and character of the use, including whether such use is of a commercial nature or is for nonprofit educational purposes

▶ The nature of the copyrighted work

▶ The amount and substantiality of the portion used in relation to the copyrighted work as a whole

▶ The effect of the use upon the potential market for which the image was intended or the value of the copyrighted work

Alteration of Work

You can alter or manipulate an image when:

▶ You have created the image yourself

▶ You have received permission from the copyright owner to do so

▶ The image is clearly in the public domain

If you appropriate or copy a recognizable image (or part of that image) that another artist has uniquely created and copyrighted, and if you don't make a good-faith attempt to obtain permission from that artist, the law clearly states that you are liable for damages, and the artist is entitled to compensation.

When in Doubt

Clearly, there will be times when releases and permissions may be impossible to obtain. There will be times when copyright owners cannot be found or when copyright is unknown or ambiguous. What do you do then?

If you decide to use an image without obtaining permission, be sure to keep a record of the steps you took to obtain permission. Keep all returned letters and phone records. Credit the picture the best you can. None of this will preclude the possibility of legal action, but it will show good faith on your part, and likely minimize any damages if a case against you is pursued.

If you have any doubts about the identity of a person in the image and are concerned about matters of privacy, you might consider using image processing software to silhouette or otherwise disguise the person's face. This holds true for possible trademark violations as well. For example, if Mickey Mouse is prominent in a key image—and knowing the sensitivity of the Disney Corporation to uses of their trademarked image—you might digitally alter the image so that Mickey is not recognizable.

Case Study:

Corbis on Copyright and Clearances (Excerpts from a conversation with legal counsel Christopher Pesce.)

Things have changed a lot since the last revision of the Copyright Act in 1976. When that act took effect in 1978, all finished creative work put in a tangible form is protected by copyright without any formalities. Copyright simply springs into existence when the work is created. A lot of people don't realize this. There are risks involved in using still imagery and all other types of content, because somewhere out there may be a copyright owner. Every time you digitize an image, put it on a CD, or publish work incorporating the image, it may be technically an infringement of copyright. As the material gets older and older, it is more and more likely to be in the public domain and the risk decreases. There are some formalities in the old copyright act that caused a lot of material to fall into the public domain unintentionally, so there is a richer store of material as you go back in time. But there is still risk in using old work. Evaluating that risk takes a little bit of judgment, a little bit of knowledge of the technical rules of copyright, and a little bit of practical experience.

Take, for example, a Matisse painting. Matisse died within the last 70 years, and his works are still protected by French copyright law. The person who made a photographic reproduction of a Matisse painting could claim a separate, independent copyright of that photograph. Now that copyright coexists with the underlying copyright of the painting. Then someone comes along and digitizes that photograph and arguably there is another layer of copyright. Someone then uses the image in a CD-ROM and there is yet another layer of copyright. All these rights holders need permission from the underlying copyright holders in order to proceed. We have this structure of permission above permission above permission, all of which needs to be in place in order for the final product to be distributed and sold without breaking any laws in any countries in any part of the world. This is a particular challenge for CD-ROMs because they are so content-rich.

Here at Corbis if we can identify every copyright holder we are happy. We are much less comfortable when we can't. Even the material we get from public domain sources we double check. We always get documentation of the agency's policies.

For a small multimedia company, one safe approach is to create everything yourself and avoid big name sources.

Keep your subject matter simple: a single personality, a single photographer. License their work and hire them to work with you. Build a title around your content, rather than building a title first and then searching for content. Whatever you do, do your homework and put in the effort to track down sources. You will never regret this.

There is a misconception that if what you are doing has an educational component you don't need to pay attention to copyright. That's not always true.

Clearing the rights of still images is relatively straightforward. Usually you'll know where to go. With music, however, the hole gets deeper. Music involves copyright by the composer, as well as separate copyright for the sound recording. Then there are the unions. These are the hidden layers. The rule of thumb for us is to start the process of clearing music earlier than for images—expecting it to take significantly longer.

When you work with a photographer's collection, it's important to find out exactly what rights the photographer really has. Many photographers work for magazines and have contracts with them. Who owns the electronic rights? Twenty years ago that wasn't an issue. It is now. Did the magazine license the images? Or did they purchase them outright? It's vital to think this out first. It is extremely difficult to negotiate from a position where you need permission and the image is integral to your project. On the other hand if you think about this beforehand, you can make a judgment as to what you can hold on to or get rid of.

Part II

Preparing the Image

 IH030280.JPG
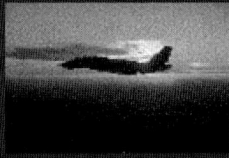 IH023437.JPG
 IH029446.JPG
 ih023072.JPG

 IH023360.JPG
 ih078633.JPG
 IH029777.JPG
 ih029881.JPG

 ih029780.JPG
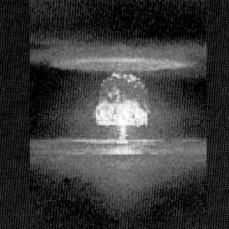 ih109113.JPG
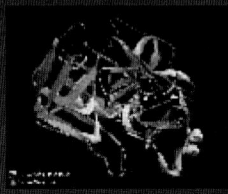 ih001082.JPG
 ih106800.JPG

 IH017574.JPG
 ih065259.JPG
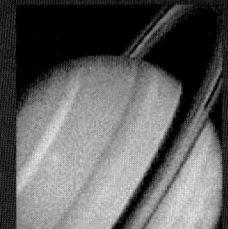 IH024697.JPG
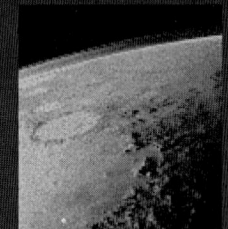 IH017576.JPG

 IH031372.JPG
 IH025247.JPG
 ih064390.JPG
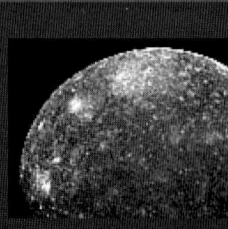 IH031387.JPG

copyright Corbis

Chapter 4

Digitizing the Image

To edit, process, and prepare an image for a multimedia presentation, an image must be in digital form—the language of the computer. Today many images are created and distributed in this form and require no further translation from the analog to the digital world. These digital images are ready for the next step, image processing, which is discussed in the following chapter.

Digital technology, however, is relatively new, and today the vast majority of existing images are not in digital form. We therefore turn to scanners, Photo CD, and other means of turning analog images into pliable mathematical equations capable of being combined seamlessly with digitized sound and text.

Converting Using Scanners, Photo CDs, and File Formats

In a glance, here are the advantages and disadvantages of the three primary ways of converting an existing analog image into a digital image.

Desktop Scanners

Desktop scanners give near instant results. If you own the equipment, you have 24-hour access, and each scan is low cost (once the scanner is paid for).

Scanners, however, are labor-intensive and require an initial outlay for hardware. They require large storage space for digital files and cannot accept large prints (typically nothing over 8 1/2"×11"). Most consumer slide scanners only scan 35mm slides and negatives, and not larger sizes.

Kodak Photo CD

Kodak Photo CDs provide low-cost storage. In addition, cost per scan ($.80–$2.00) is reasonable and they display on every TV set in the world, as well as on most computer systems. Images are scanned in multiple formats and resolutions.

Unless you have your own in-house photo CD scanning system, however, the work has to be sent or brought to an outside service provider. This takes time, and valuable content leaves your direct control. The service is only for 35mm negatives or slides. 2 1/4"×2 1/4" and 4"×5" transparency scanning is available, but for a premium cost. It also doesn't do flat art.

Service Bureaus and Other Outside Services

The advantages of using a service bureau is that you do not need to acquire expensive equipment that rapidly becomes technologically out of date. With a service bureau, you have access to an expert who can advise and make suggestions on technical matters.

The disadvantages of using a service bureau include cost, time, and the fact you must give up original art temporarily.

Scanners

Several types of scanners are available, but by far the most popular and useful among multimedia producers are the flatbed and the slide scanners.

Scanners generally are rated by their capability to discern detail (in dots per inch or dpi), and their capability to discern the tone or color of the resolved dot (rated in bits). Lower cost scanners—between $400 and $1,000—typically offer optical resolution in the range of 300–600 dpi with 24-bit color, which is sufficient for most multimedia applications. Some flatbed scanners come with adapters that allow for slide or negative scanning at resolutions adequate for multimedia applications, but not for quality print output.

Specialized 35mm slide scanners generally cost more than flatbed scanners, but scan at much higher resolutions. The Polaroid Sprint Scan 35, for example, costs around $1,800 and scans 24-bit files in resolutions up to 2700 dpi.

Besides resolution and bit depth, the speed in which a scanner scans is an important consideration, especially if your multimedia projects use a lot of digitized images.

Scanners are controlled by software that performs a variety of functions, such as saving the image in various generic file formats, brightness, contrast and color balance controls, and image scaling. Software controls also provide tools that allow you to manipulate the image's gamma curve for precise tonal control.

Scanning Tips

Scanning requires experimentation. While the hardware and software do most of the work, there are some things that you can do to ensure that the best possible scan is realized from your image. Recognizing that the setup differs from flatbed scanners to slide scanners, here are some tips.

▶ Start with a well-exposed and printed photograph. If scanning from a halftone source, expect strange repetitive patterns called *moiré*, which are caused by divergent angles of the sensing device and the halftone dots. This anomaly can be corrected either by moving the image on the scanner and rescanning, scanning it slightly out of focus, or by using image processing software at a later time.

▶ It's not a disaster if an image is scanned at the wrong angle because most imaging software will correct for this. However, because rotating an image requires intense mathematical calculations and is therefore time-consuming, it's best to take an extra moment and make sure that the image's horizon line is adjusted to the correct angle.

▶ There are advantages to scanning the image at a spatial resolution that closely matches the capabilities of the display device. (Typically 72 pixels per inch [ppi] for a Macintosh monitor and 96 ppi for an IBM-compatible PC monitor.) This keeps image files as small and manageable as possible and saves operator time on the scanner. However, if your scanner has the capabilities and if you have enough data storage space, it's beneficial to scan at least double the final spatial and tonal resolution. This gives you enough "data" in case you need to crop or otherwise process the image.

▶ Most scanning software will help you determine the scanning resolution (ppi or dpi) you need. If not, you can figure it out yourself. Take the longest dimension of the final image size (for a typical Macintosh monitor this would be 640 pixels) and multiply this number by the screen resolution (typically 72 ppi). Now take your original image (for example a 5"×7" glossy photograph) and multiply the longest dimension of the image (7") by the screen resolution (72 ppi). Divide the result (504) into the results of your first calculations (46080). The resulting number will be the ppi that you need to scan your image at to exactly fill your screen. In the example, this number is 91 ppi or dpi (46080 divided by 504 = 91). Remember, it's always a good idea to double this number if you have sufficient storage space.

▶ Many vintage black–and–white images are toned and actually contain some subtle color. Scan and save the image in color to preserve the original look and feel of toned "black-and-white" images.

▶ To save time and unnecessary intermediate steps, save your images in a file format—such as TIFF or PICT—that your image processing software or presentation software is capable of opening.

▶ Photoshop and other image processing software make it easy to despeckle or rid an image of dust spots and "noise" caused by the scanning process. I have always found it worth the time, however, to take an extra second and carefully clean both the scanner and original print/negative/slide. I use lint-free swatches, compressed air, and an emulsion cleaner.

▶ A typical flatbed scanner will accept two–dimensional art up to 8 1/2 ×11 inches (more expensive units will take up to 11×17 inches). Most slide scanners typically only accept 35mm slides or negatives. Because negatives, slides, and prints come in a variety of sizes, there may be times when you need to use an outside service that has more sophisticated equipment than you have available. Another option is to convert your oversized print (or negative/transparency) to a 35mm copy slide or negative. You can do this yourself, or you can take the material to a photo lab. Digitizing is easier and less expensive once you have your work in a 35mm format.

Going Digital with Eastman Kodak's Photo CD

Kodak's Photo CD merges the best of the analog and digital worlds. Photo CD is both a technical standard for describing and storing images, and a product line that includes scanning hardware and specially equipped CD players that enable you to play back your image on a common TV set or a computer monitor. If you have a CD-ROM drive that is compatible with the Photo CD format (and most are) you need not buy any hardware. Literally thousands of service bureaus across the country will take your negative or slide, digitize it, and put it on a CD. Prices for 35mm (color negative or slide) vary from $.80 a scan to a few dollars. Larger sized negatives and transparencies such as 2 1/4"×2 1/4" or 4"×5" require a special Pro Photo CD scan, which at 4096×6144 pixels gives you much higher resolution than you'll likely ever need for multimedia work. Each Pro Photo CD scan runs around $15. The discs cost only a few dollars. You can store over 100 images on a regular Photo CD and about 25 images on a Pro Photo CD.

NOTE   Kodak also offers a Photo CD Portfolio Disc that enables you to publish your own multimedia presentations complete with images, stereo audio, graphics, text, and interactive capabilities. More on that in Chapter 7, "The Electronic Canvas: Design and Software Tools for the New Media."

Images are stored in Kodak's proprietary YCC format, which separates color images into a luminance (brightness) component and two chroma (color) components. Using a special technique, a single image can be stored in up to six different resolutions using a minimum of disc space. (Image Pacs, as the separate files are called, only save the color data once at "Base" resolution and save the luminance data for each resolution.)

These resolutions, including the Pro scan, are:

▶ Base/16. 192×192 pixels for a file size of 72 KB. Good for thumbnail images.

▶ Base/4. 256×384 for a file size of 288 KB. Good for multimedia and Web purposes at a maximum size of 3.5"×5" on-screen.

▶ Base. 512×384 for a file size of 1.12 MB. Good for full-screen multimedia and Web purposes.

▶ Base 4. 1024×1536 for a file size of 4.5 MB. Full-screen images for high-definition TV.

▶ Base 16. 2048×3072 for a file size of 18 MB. More than you need for multimedia purposes.

▶ Base 64(Pro only). 4096×6144 pixels for a file size of 72 MB. Much more than you need for multimedia purposes, but great for magazine prints.

Most of the latest versions of imaging software programs will open Kodak's proprietary YCC format. Photoshop 3.0, for example, comes with a Kodak Photo CD Acquire Plug-in Module that enables you to open any of the resolutions present, and to choose between RGB and Lab color workspace. Once open, the image file can be saved in any of the several formats that Photoshop supports. However, you cannot save files in the Photo CD format. A plug-in acquire module also is available from Kodak that gives you a choice of image sharpening, color space, and resolution changes on-the-fly, for more precise image enhancements.

NOTE   If your application software doesn't read the Photo CD format—and a lot of the older versions such as Painter 3.0 don't—you'll need special software to translate the format into one you can use. Two such software programs are Access Plus by Kodak and DeBabelizer by Equilibrium.

The quality of the Photo CD scan will ultimately depend on the quality of the actual image, the type of film you use, and who performs the scan. Kodak has devoted a lot of time and energy into improving the Photo CD system, creating better import software, and working with imaging companies to improve the interface. Among users who use Photo CD for print media, there have been complaints about the conversion of Photo CD files into CMYK, the necessary color space for color printing. In general, for multimedia purposes, I've been happy with the scans I've gotten from a variety of sources. This doesn't mean that the images are perfect and ready to be placed in a multimedia application. I always use Photoshop to color enhance the images, for example, increasing the saturation and lowering the overall gamma.

When sending images out to be scanned, follow these guidelines:

▶ Carefully clean your slides or negatives before you take them in. Some Photo CD labs are more careful than others. It's a drag getting digitized images back with dust spots that need to be processed out.

▶ Inform the operator what type of film you were using, such as Fujichrome, Ektachrome, or Extapress. Each film has its own characteristics and Photo CD equipment that can be adjusted to take those into consideration.

▶ When you can, use a local Photo CD lab. If this isn't an option for logistical or economic reasons, use an overnight delivery service to ensure safe delivery of your valuable images. Package your material carefully in archival sleeves and protect it with bubble wrap or cardboard.

NOTE　　To find the closest Photo CD service near you, call (800) 23 Kodak, or look in the Yellow Pages under Photo Finishing.

▶ Shop around for a Photo CD Lab that will give you a good price as well as good service. Some labs charge as little as $.80 a scan, while others charge $2.50 for the same service. Most labs charge less for large orders.

Other Photo CD-Type Services

There are other services similar to Photo CD, whereby you send a print, negative, or slide and receive a digital file in return. Most of them are oriented toward the consumer market, returning digital files on a floppy disk or even online. Picture Place, available on AOL, is one such service. Others are listed in the appendix. If you choose to use any of these services, make sure you are getting a digital file with resolution high enough for your needs and in a convenient file format.

Frame-Grabbing from Video

Moving video, such as a VHS tape and broadcast television, contain up to 30 frames (or 60-interlaced fields) of still images per second, with each frame containing about 640×480 pixels at 24-bits of image information. Any one of these frames can be "grabbed" directly from a VCR, a television broadcast, or a camcorder by the use of special equipment. The actual quality of this still image will vary depending on the quality of the videotape, the quality of the broadcast, and the quality of the equipment you use to grab the frame. With a little image processing, the frame is usually suitable for multimedia purposes. (Processing is covered in Chapter 5, "Image Processing.")

Standard video is by nature *analog*, which means the image is saved as electronic waves rather than as discrete digital numbers. To use a video image you must first digitize it, and to do this you need a video digitizing board and software. (Newer digital video systems don't need analog to digital conversion.)

Onboard video digitizers are included in some computers (usually designated as AV models). Add-on video digitizing boards—sold by such companies as Radius and TrueVision—can be purchased separately. Most boards handle both composite and S-video signals. Composite signals include both brightness and color information as one signal. S-video produces better quality, because the color and brightness are separated into two different signals. The best quality standard is component video, where the video signal is broken down into two separate colors and one brightness component. Component video is only associated with professional video equipment, and only the most expensive video digitizing boards can work with this signal.

Most video digitizing boards are designed to digitize full-motion video, a tricky, time-consuming, and memory-intensive process. Grabbing stills poses few technical challenges, and for that reason lower-cost digitizers with fewer features can be used with no problem. Most come with software capable of saving files in either PICT or TIFF formats.

When a digitizing board "grabs" a frame of video, it is actually grabbing two sequential fields. A *field* contains every other horizontal line in a frame. These lines become interlaced with the subsequent field to create one image.

Keep in mind the following when grabbing a frame:

▶ Grabbing a frame from a video is like shooting a camera with a sticky trigger. There is a lag between the time you "click" the shutter and the moment the frame is grabbed. If you don't get the frame you wanted, you can rewind and start over. Nothing is lost except time.

▶ Because of the limited color spectrum of video, you'll need to do some color correction and processing to optimize the image.

▶ To de-interlace and further clean the image, use Photoshop's de-interlace filter.

Other Ways of Digitizing

The following are other ways of digitizing images that are relatively inexpensive and might be appropriate for some multimedia projects.

Still Video Cameras

A number of years ago, before digital cameras became widely available, Sony, Canon, Casio, and other mostly Japanese manufacturers offered still video cameras. These cameras, which are still available, produce an NTSC video signal, stored on a 2" floppy disk. Each frame contains a 24-bit color, 640×480 pixel image. Since these cameras output a video analog signal, they must be used in conjunction with a video digitizer. Because of low resolution, the cameras enjoyed only limited success. However, they are perfect for multimedia applications, and they can be found at bargain prices.

Desktop Digitizers

QuickCam is a tiny video camera that fits on your desk and records only black-and-white images (320×240 pixels) and sound directly into the computer at a cost of less than $100. In recent years there has been a proliferation of similar devices, making it easier than ever to add an image to email or to an electronic document. Handheld scanners and small desktop scanners, such as Storm's EasyPhoto Reader, fall into this category of low-cost digitizing devices.

Fax Machines

Fax machines actually are digitizers that can be used in a pinch. Many fax machines actually transmit a limited amount of grayscale information. You can fax an image to your computer's fax/modem, and then convert the file into a format compatible with your image processing software.

File Formats

Figuring out ways to go from one file format to another is a major issue among multimedia producers. More than 50 different graphic file formats are available, including TIFF, JPEG, EPS, IVUE, WMF, and YCC (the propriety format developed by Kodak for their Photo CD process). A producer might receive material in any of these formats and then must convert the file into a format that he or she can use.

Simply put, file formats organize the data that describe digital images. Some of these formats can only be used by a specific application and are called native formats. Others are more standardized, and allow inter-application movement, such as TIFF and JPEG. Commercial content providers generally use cross-platform and cross-application file formats: TIFF for standard image files, and JPEG for images delivered online.

Most graphics software accepts a variety of file formats and has the capability to convert and save digital image into other file formats. If you are working with a digital image in Photoshop, for example, you may want to convert the image from a TIFF to a Photoshop-native format. This native format creates a smaller file size using a special compression technique that enables the software to process the image much more efficiently. When you are finished processing or manipulating the image in Photoshop, you can reconvert it to a TIFF format and output the file to a multimedia application program, such as Director.

Also available is so-called file translator software, which turns PICT files into TIFF files readable by both Macs and PCs.

DeBabelizer is probably the most used software application for converting files into formats that can be read by different application programs and different computer platforms. It is a commercial product available for both the PC and Macintosh. It is not only a format converter, but also a batch processor that automates the file conversion process. A producer who needs to convert hundreds of images can set up DeBabelizer, go away for the evening, and return the next day to a finished job.

Other specialized translating software also is available, some of which is shareware. (See the appendix for more information.)

Working with Service Bureaus

To save the expense and hassle of buying and operating a scanner, or to make scans of large prints or negatives, turn to specially equipped service bureaus. Service bureaus are like overnight print shops, and range from small operations catering to the needs of desktop publishers to large firms serving ad agencies and professional publishing houses. Quality, services, and prices vary accordingly. (A partial list is available in the appendix.)

When working with a service bureau, ask the following questions:

▶ How organized is the service bureau? Can they meet your deadline? Might they lose your material? Word of mouth is your best source of information.

▶ Will the service bureau negotiate prices? They are more likely to do so if you are bringing them quantity or if you have a loose deadline.

▶ What type of equipment do they use? Are they up-to-date, or are they stuck with older, less efficient equipment that will not do a good job?

NOTE   Service bureaus also are great places to find out about the latest software or hardware and to get information that otherwise might be difficult to find. These tidbits might come from a fellow customer who, like you, is waiting for service or from one of the service bureau's employees who confronts the reality of incompatible hardware and buggy software on a daily basis.

IH025739.JPG ih052553.JPG ih052593.JPG ih001387.JPG

ih044018.JPG IH012769.JPG ih044014.JPG ih064229.JPG

IH025761.JPG ih065299.JPG IH017808.JPG ih044033.JPG

ih044032.JPG IH018261.JPG IH012959.JPG ih069763.JPG

RT001178.JPG RT001301.JPG ih069795.JPG RT001308.JPG

Chapter 5

Image Processing

Image processing will make its appearance in any project. You will almost always have to either process or resize your digital images. Even the images that are contained on the accompanying CD-ROM—optimized for use in electronic presentations and titles—will likely need to be customized for your particular project.

Although image processing has a daunting sound to it—I always think of scientists with thick-rimmed glasses huddled over super computers processing digital images relayed to earth from a NASA probe orbiting Jupiter—software such as Adobe's Photoshop and Equilibrium's DeBabelizer have made much of the work easy and intuitive. You only need to learn the common tasks and which software to use when.

Keep in mind the distinction between image processing and image manipulation that was discussed in Chapter 2, "Creating Your Own Images." Chapter 2 discussed making gross changes to an image, using image editing tools such as airbrushes, cut-and-paste, and using clone tools where pixels are actually added and content is changed. For our purposes, image processing can be thought of as enhancing or bringing out the best qualities of an existing image. It means optimizing an image's tonal qualities; cleaning up dust, scratches, and electronic noise created by the scanning process, and perhaps most importantly, matching both the spatial and tonal resolution to a particular display system. A properly processed image will not only look great on a monitor, but will also have neither too much nor too little data, thereby optimizing transmission speed and minimizing storage space.

It's tempting to say that image processing is more a technical process than image manipulation, but in fact there is an art to getting it just right, which will require experimentation. The care one puts into this process will be reflected in the final outcome. The works of DCI and Corbis, two companies who put great emphasis on quality of the digital image, demonstrate how stunning the final outcome can be.

Display Systems

Display systems, which are the ultimate destination for our digital images, are not all alike. They differ in size and display capabilities. Even if you make an assumption about what equipment your audience may use to view your work—for example a 13" cathode ray tube (CRT) monitor, capable of displaying 8-bit color—you have no control over how the image will actually look on their system. There are many variables, including: the amount and quality of ambient light; monitor brightness and contrast control settings; monitor color temperature settings (from 4100 degrees Kelvin to 7500 degrees Kelvin); and color calibration used, if any. In addition, display systems, especially ones using CRT technology, are notoriously fickle. Monitors vary from model to model, from manufacturer to manufacturer, and from day to day because of changing temperature and the aging of the phosphorous tube. They even change if the monitor is rotated relative to magnetic north!

How then does one create an image that looks the same on all monitors? You can't. It's virtually impossible. However, there are certain things you can do that will make your images look good on most display systems.

To start, make sure your monitor is working at its peak performance. To do this on a typical CRT computer display system, follow these steps:

▶ Calibrate your monitor by using a combination of software and hardware. If your system doesn't have these features, you can at least physically adjust the brightness and contrast controls that all monitors have to visually pleasing levels.

▶ If it is an option, set the color temperature of your monitor to 6500 degrees K, the most common color temperature. (I prefer working with the warmer 5000 degrees K, which approximates the color of white under sunlight at noon, but few consumer monitors can display this temperature.)

▶ Regularly degauss your monitor to remove the effects of magnetic pulls that make the images on the monitor look wavy.

▶ Have the original art in front of you for comparison.

▶ When you are finished, find the crummiest display system you can find, and as a reality check, look at your digital file on it.

Having said all this, keep in mind that the human eye is very forgiving. When we look at a monitor, our expectations are lower than if we look at a printed page. Because most display systems are backlit, this helps create an illusion of quality similar to looking at slides. Also, our brain quickly compensates for slight color shifts; for example, it makes an image with an overall bluish cast appear normal.

Now what?

After you've calibrated your monitor, open your image file by using image processing software such as Photoshop. (Photoshop is the best all-around image-processing program, but for certain specific tasks such as creating custom color palettes, DeBabelizer offers more options, but more on that later.) If you have the option, and want to replicate the original as closely as possible, set a copy of the original image next to the screen for comparison. Look at the image on the screen and determine what needs to be done. Some flaws such as scratches, dust, and artifacts left over from the scanning process, and an unwanted color cast will be obvious to the eye. Other factors such as contrast or lack thereof, color balance, and saturation are best determined by the use of one of Photoshop's various analyzing tools (that is, the histogram). This is explained in more detail later.

After you have identified the problems associated with a particular image, you can select one or more of the following methods:

▶ Despeckle to rid the image of small random artifacts.

▶ Use tonal control to optimize contrast and dynamic range.

▶ Remove unwanted color casts and increase/decrease color saturation.

▶ Match both spatial and tonal resolution to desired output.

▶ Create a custom color palette.

▶ Change the frame and pixel aspect. (Relevant only if going between different platforms.)

The order in which you carry out these tasks can vary. Generally, the last things you do are tasks that throw away the most data, tasks such as resizing and resampling. However, there are times—for example, when you are working with an 18 MB or larger file—that it makes sense to do some preliminary resizing to make the image easier to work with. Always save the original high-resolution file separately for other purposes, such as creating new images at different resolutions.

NOTE   If you are preparing an image for use on the Web or to be transmitted, compression is always the last thing you'll do. This is because most compression techniques result in some irretrievable data loss. More on compression in the next chapter.

Case Study:

DCI on Processing Images

(Mac McCall, chief engineer for Digital Collections Incorporated, the publisher of the award-winning Mapplethorpe CD-ROM, discusses image processing.)

"The first thing I look for in an image is dynamic range, whether the dark areas are totally without information—or whether I can bring out something there, and particularly the white and brighter areas, to make sure that there is still some information in those places. I can then manipulate the image toward those goals, then follow up with a quick cleanup. Good scans generally don't need a lot of cleanup. Often I need to increase the overall tonal saturation. Then, at that point, I apply some degree of unsharp masking to 'crisp' up the image. It is important not to overdo the unsharp masking or you'll end up with an artificial-looking image. These are essentially the steps I go through for each image. Of course, an individual image might have its own specific problem that I need to fix. For example, it might need to be cropped, resized, or rotated."

Despeckling

I've never seen a scanned image that doesn't contain either dust marks or a stray pixel or two caused by electronic "noise." Thankfully, it is easy to rid images of these distractions.

Using Photoshop, select the area you want to clean up. Under the Filter menu, choose Noise. You'll then have four options to choose from: Add Noise, Despeckle, Dust & Scratches, and Median. Forget Add Noise and choose one of the other three. Despeckle diminishes noise by subtly blurring an image. However, detail is preserved because this filter blurs everything except the edges in an image, where significant shifts in color occur. I find this filter most useful for removing the moiré patterns that sometimes occur when scanning halftone art and for "cleaning up" grabbed video frames.

For more control use the Dust & Scratches option. By using the Radius and Threshold level sliders in conjunction with this option, you can determine the size of the dust or scratch that will be removed and how different the value of the dust or scratch needs to be before it is eliminated or altered. If the Radius setting is too high or the Threshold setting too low, the image will appear out of focus. It's best to apply this filter to specific areas of the image that are in need of work. Remember, if you apply something you don't like, you can simply select the Undo command in the Edit menu.

The Median filter blends the brightness of pixels and discards pixels that are radically different from adjacent pixels. The Radius slider controls determine how much variation in brightness values the filter will look for. Too high a value causes a blurred image.

I find it most useful to use these filters in conjunction with the Rubber stamp tool found in the toolbox. I use this tool in areas of detail to duplicate the pixels surrounding an offensive scratch or unwanted mark and "clone" over it. I save the Dust & Scratches filter for areas of the image that are lacking in detail, such as skies, or other broad expanses of similar color and tone. The Smudge and Blur tools usually are not good alternatives because they smear and blend pixels and create an unrealistic effect.

(It's usually at this stage of image processing that I spot out "red eye," the distracting phenomena that occurs when a person is photographed in the dark with a direct flash. Here, the Smudge and Blur tools come in handy.)

NOTE   Many historical photos and images have scratches. If you want to keep the authentic historical look and feel, don't apply this stage of processing to them.

Tonal Control: Optimizing Contrast and Dynamic Range

Contrast is determined by the relationships between pixels. The more variation between adjacent pixels, the more apparent contrast. The less variation, the less apparent contrast, resulting in an image that can look dull or flat to the eye. *Dynamic range* expresses the distribution of tonal qualities throughout the spectrum. An image with low dynamic range will contain few if any details in the shadows and highlights.

Contrast and dynamic range are determined by the original image and the quality of the scan that created the digital file. The better the original image and the better the scan, the less work you have to do to optimize the image quality.

While it is possible to visibly determine what corrections need to be done, for more precision use Photoshop's histogram (under the Image menu). The histogram graphically represents tonal distribution in an image. High contrast images show up as two peaks on the graph at either end of the brightness area. Low contrast images show up as a mound in only one region of the graph.

If measurements show pixels falling between a small portion of gray values and none in other areas, there is a small dynamic range present. A wide distribution shows a large dynamic range.

The next step, after determining what needs to be done, is to use one of Photoshop's several tonal control commands found under the Image menu. These commands are as follows:

▶ Equalize (under the Map submenu)

▶ Levels (under the Adjust submenu)

▶ Curves (under the Adjust submenu)

▶ Brightness/Contrast (under the Adjust submenu)

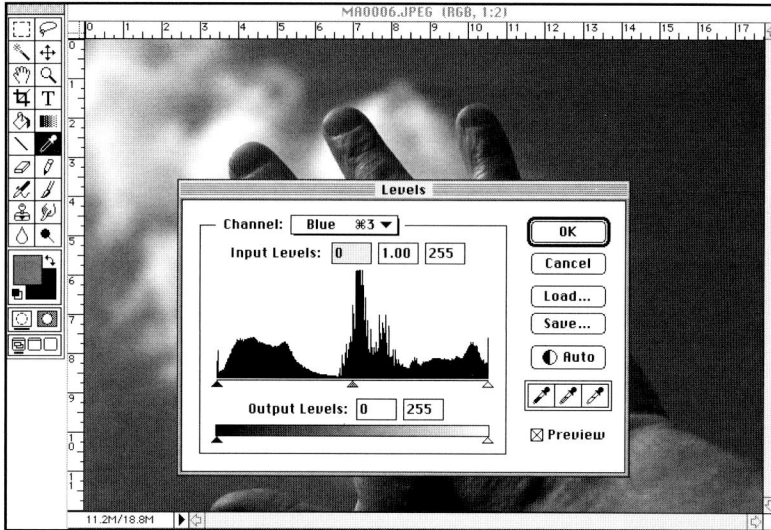

Figure 5.1 Photoshop's Levels control.

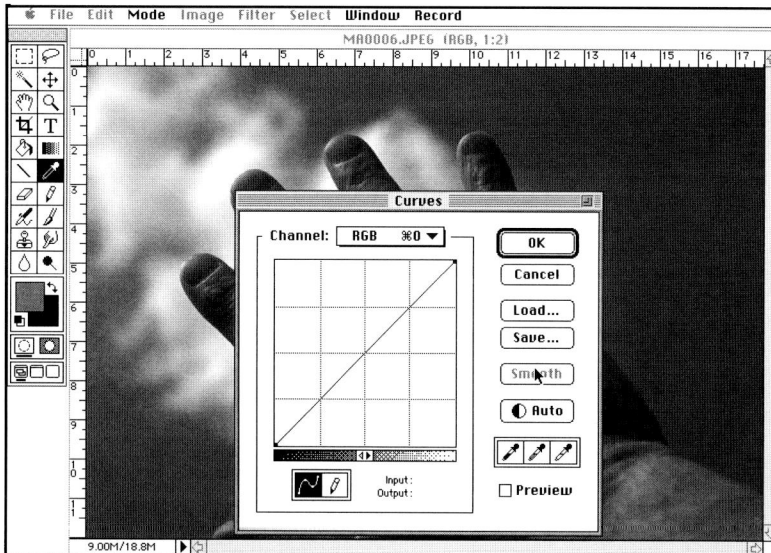

Figure 5.2 Photoshop's Curves control.

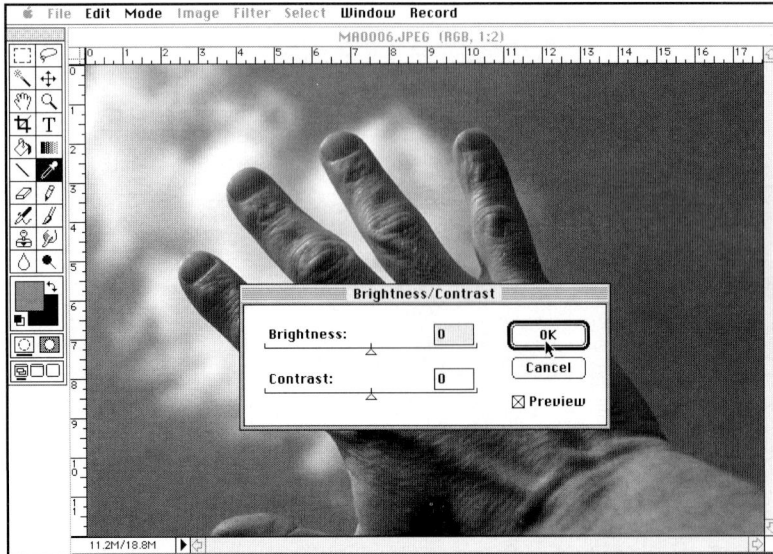

Figure 5.3   Photoshop's Brightness/Contrast controls.

The Equalize control balances the brightness and contrast values by setting the darkest value to black, the brightness value to white, and redistributes the other values to an even range of tones. Levels enable you to set the highlight, midtone, and shadow values. Curves provide a visual graph that enables you to adjust not only the highlight, midtone, and shadow values, but also any value at any point on the graph. The Brightness/Contrast control is the easiest to use—contrast sliders affect the relationships between pixels, making an adjacent pixel, for example, brighter, while making another darker, and brightness sliders affect all the pixels equally—but it only offers limited control over the image.

As you experiment with these tools, watch as they apply their changes in real time to the image on the screen. Don't think only in terms of keeping detail in the shadow and highlight areas. Consider the overall look and feel of the image. Sometimes a high contrast image with the highlights burned out is what works. Also keep in mind that Photoshop can only improve a poorly exposed or scanned image up to a point, which is why the original quality of the image and scan are so important.

Of all the tonal control tools, I find the Curves and Levels tools the most useful. They give me much more control over the image.

NOTE   If you are processing a batch of images that are destined to be shown together, be consistent. Stay in the same ballpark with contrast, tonal, and saturation.

Removing Unwanted Color Casts and Increase/Decrease Color Saturation

Color casts may be a result of poor scanning or they may be inherent in the original image. In either case, it is an issue whenever you don't like it. (Eggs, for example, are not very appetizing when they are presented with a sick greenish cast—an effect that might have been caused by shooting color film under fluorescent lighting conditions). *Color saturation* is the intensity of hue of a particular color. Images with low color saturation will simply appear washed out and lack their potential richness and attractiveness.

Again, Photoshop provides several commands—both automatic and manual—for removing color casts and increasing or decreasing color saturation. Remember that by using the Selection tool you always have the option of applying color changes to specific areas of the image (local) or to the entire image (global).

Auto correction commands are all found under Image in the main menu bar. The quickest auto correction is Auto levels, but Auto correction also is found under the submenu Adjust under Levels or Curves. Auto correction not only attempts to create pure white and pure black and adjust the color range, but also attempts to balance the color cast by adjusting the RGB components of the image. Remember that auto correction will work on all or a selected part of the image. If your image still contains a black border be sure to either remove this border or only work on a selection within the black border. The border fools Photoshop's auto correction tools into thinking the image is darker than it is.

Manual correction can be done several ways using the tools under the Image menu and Adjust submenu. For quick, global color correction use the Levels and Curves tools. To remove unwanted color casts, use the Color Balance command, which adjusts the balance of colors in the image. Use the Hue/Saturation command to make global or selective color changes to the color tint (hue), purity of color (saturation), or the lightness of the color. Replace

Color and Selective Color commands allow for even more selective and precise color correction.

Keep in mind that a color image is made up of Red, Green, and Blue layers of color. Using the Levels and Curves command, you can select and control any one of these colors and therefore affect the entire image.

Variations is another handy Photoshop command option also found under the Image menu. This command allows you to visually adjust an image's color balance, contrast, and saturation. As you click on small color correct previews, the original image changes accordingly. Optional sample corrections are also included.

I almost always use the Curves command. First I try auto correction and see what that does. Then, if I am not satisfied, I find the midpoint of the curve, click and then rotate the point in a circle until I get the color correction I want. I also frequently use the Variations command.

Frankly, I find color correction to be like a black hole—I go in but don't seem to come out. It's so easy to overdo color corrections, especially when you consider that color is subjective and everyone perceives colors a bit differently. Remember your results will vary from monitor to monitor anyway.

Matching Spatial and Tonal Resolution

There are two types of resolution that must be matched: spatial and tonal. *Spatial resolution* simply expresses the total number of pixels or dots that make up an image. *Tonal resolution* usually means the maximum number of color (or tonal) possibilities per pixel.

Matching Spatial Resolution

Most monitors are capable of displaying only 72 pixels per square inch. Unless you are planning to display your work on a monitor with different characteristics, any resolution higher than this is a waste and will only create a larger file size with no increase in quality.

To check or change the image resolution look under Photoshop's Image menu and select Image Size. Verify that 72 is present under the resolution number heading. If not, simply enter 72 (or any number that matches your output devices capabilities). Make sure that the file size box in the lower right is not checked when you change your resolution.

The amount of resizing that you apply to your images will depend both on the size you want the image to appear on the screen and the capabilities of the monitor on which the work is likely to be seen. Most multimedia producers assume their viewers will see their work on a 13" monitor which has a maximum resolution of 640×480 pixels. If you resize an image to these specifications, keep in mind that on a screen capable of displaying a greater resolution the image will fill only a small part of the screen or, if blown-up, will look pixilated.

Resizing is also done under the Image menu, Image Size. Photoshop's default setting shows the image size in inches, but it is more useful to view the size in pixels. If you want to maintain your image's original aspect ratio you have to select Proportion instead of File size.

Keep in mind that when you use Photoshop to resize an image, the program does this by interpolating data. This means that Photoshop fills in data that is missing by making an educated guess. Under the General Preferences submenu you will find options for telling Photoshop exactly how to do this: Nearest Neighbor, Bilinear, or Bicubic. For the most part, Nearest Neighbor is the most accurate method, especially for continuous tone images.

Matching Tonal Resolution

Here again, you need to know or assume the characteristics of the monitor and the video graphics card you intend the work to be viewed on. A typical 8-bit video card attached to a typical color monitor can display 256 colors or shades of gray. More and more computer systems are being shipped with 16-bit video display cards which are capable of displaying 16,384 colors. High-end graphics display systems use 24-bit video display cards which are capable of displaying 16.8 million colors—many more than the human eye can discern.

As in spatial resolution, preparing an image that contains too much tonal resolution is a waste. All those extra colors won't be appreciated or even seen by someone who has a system only capable of viewing 8 bits of color. (If you have a display system that allows you to switch color depth on-the-fly, you can see what I mean. Open a 24-bit image and see what it looks like in 8-bit color.)

Most images you are likely to work with start as 24-bit images. (This includes all the images on the accompanying CD-ROM.) In order to redefine this number so that your image will be optimized for monitors that display less colors, you'll need to apply a process called color indexing. Color indexing discards color information (which is irretrievable); it tries to make up for the lost colors by juxtaposing two or more similar colors through the use of a color palette that defines which colors will be used and dithering (see below).

Again, using Photoshop, choose Indexed Color under the Mode menu. Here you can chose the appropriate resolution, ranging from 3 bits/pixel to 8 bits/pixel. You'll have the following five types of color palettes from which to choose:

▶ Exact palette. Use Exact palette only if the image you are working with has 256 or fewer colors.

▶ System palette. Use the System palette if you are not sure which palette you want to use.

▶ Adaptive palettes. Use Adaptive palettes when you want a palette that is specially created to optimize the colors in a particular image. This is your best bet when you are converting a 24-bit image to an 8-bit one.

▶ Custom palette. Use Custom palette when you want to create your own color table.

▶ Previous palette. Use Previous palette when you want to apply the same palette to subsequent images.

You also have a choice whether to dither. *Dithering* is a process which mixes available colors to simulate a wider range of colors or, in the case of a grayscale image, creates the appearance of shades of gray. Dithering creates a smooth, natural-looking gradation between adjacent colors, rather than the sharp contrast between colors (called banding) that often results from resampling to fewer colors. In Photoshop, you have two ways to do this: Diffusion and Pattern dither. Diffusion gives a more natural, random arrangement of pixels, while Pattern gives a rigid, grid-like appearance to the image. (You can only choose Pattern when you have chosen System palette.) Both methods of dithering result in an image that looks grainy, but doesn't have the banding that often results when a 24-bit image is reduced to 8 or fewer bits.

In general, dithering is very useful because it optimizes the imaging capability of the hardware. But a dithered image is sometimes such a complex lattice-work of real and interpolated values that it becomes almost impossible to edit or resize the image. When resized or otherwise manipulated, a dithered image pixelizes into artificial patterns and clumps. Therefore, before applying a dithering technique be sure that you have carried out all your other image processing steps and have sized the image to the correct size. Dithering is not recommended if you plan to convert your images to video and show them on a TV where they will shimmer or flicker more than other images. Dithering should also be avoided when preparing images for use on the Web, but more on that in Chapter 9, "Still Images on the Web."

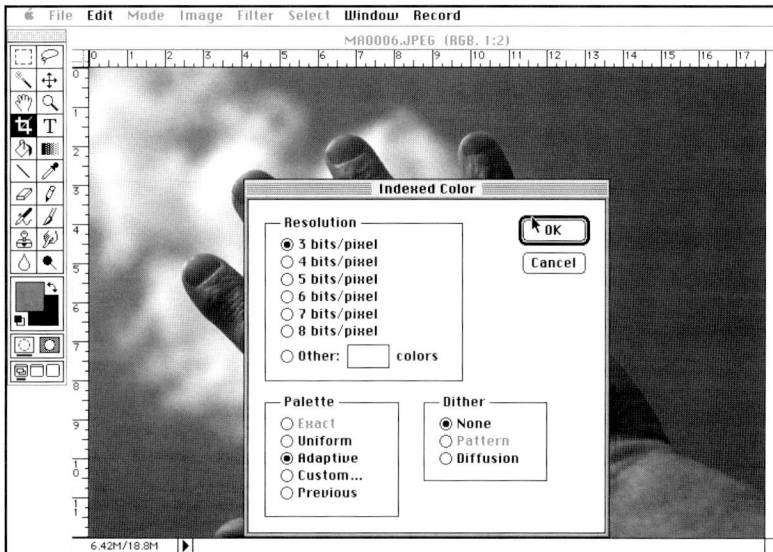

Figure 5.4 Photoshop's Indexed Color options.

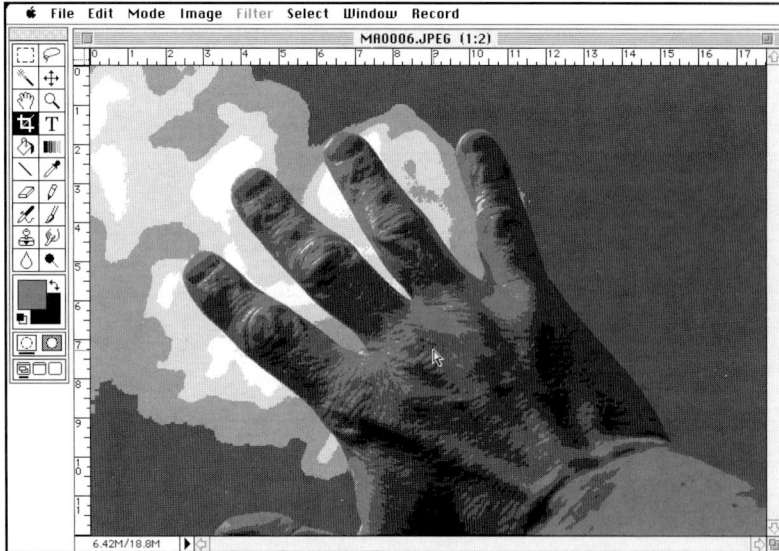

Figure 5.5   3 bits per pixel, Adaptive Palette.

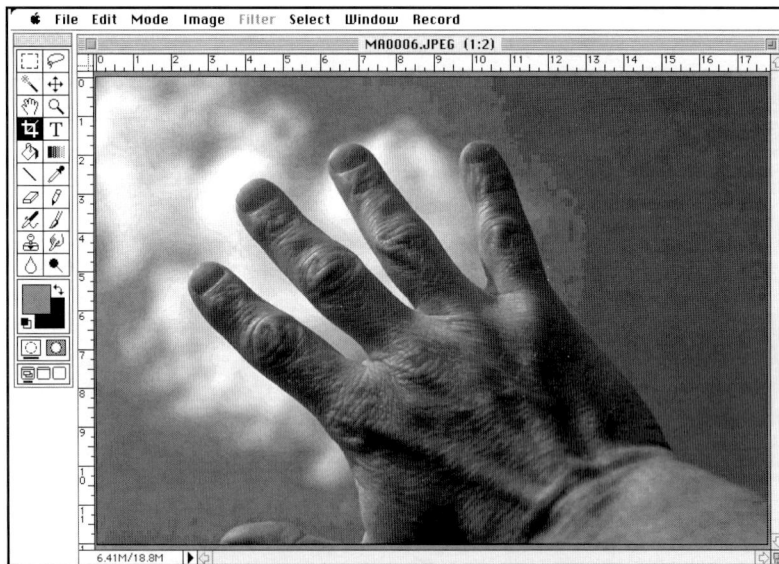

Figure 5.6   8 bits per pixel, Adaptive Palette.

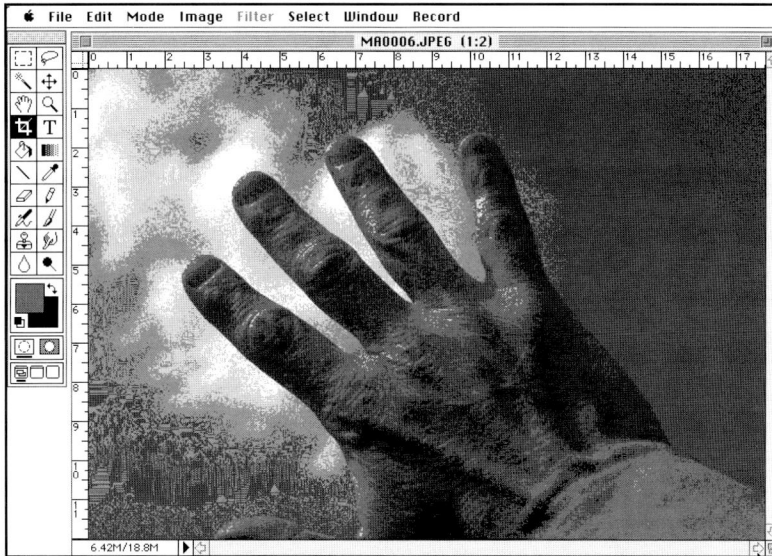

Figure 5.7   3 bits per pixel, Adaptive Palette with Diffusion Dither.

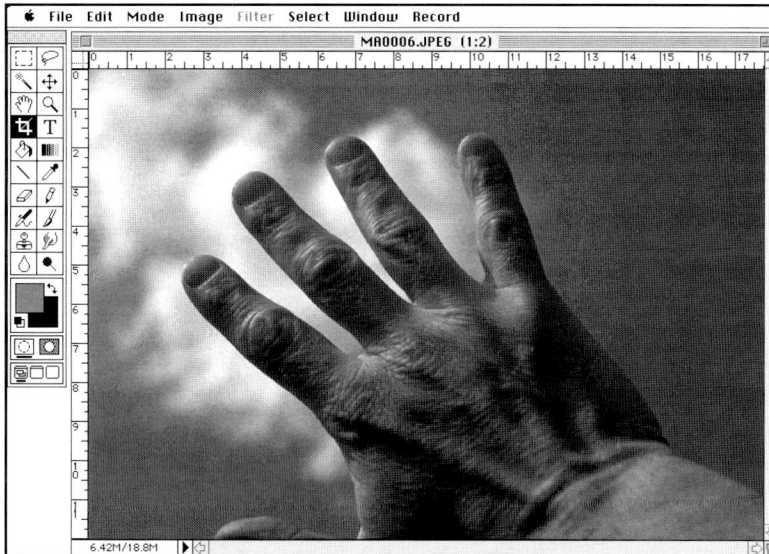

Figure 5.8   8 bits per pixel, Adaptive Palette with Diffusion Dither.

As mentioned earlier, you might want to consider using Equilibrium's DeBabelizer to create custom palettes and apply dithering techniques. DeBabelizer gives you many more options than Photoshop. For example, you have two choices of ways to dither (Albie Dither, which results in higher contrast and Diffusion Dither which is more normal looking) and you can determine the percentage of dithering as well as select certain areas of the image to dither. This is especially useful if you have a background that you want to look smooth and natural. You simply choose Don't Dither Background Color.

NOTE   If you have multiple images that all require similar processing, such as Despeckle, Sharpen, and Resize, use software such as DeBabelizer or PhotoMatic from DayStar. Both programs allow you to create a script that automates any repetitive task. Processing can occur in the background or be programmed to run overnight.

NOTE   Many multimedia professionals prefer to use Equilibrium Technologies' DeBabelizer to process images. DeBabelizer—the name is derived from the Biblical story of the Tower of Babel—is not as easy to use as Photoshop, but in certain respects it offers more options and control. It can batch process a series of images at once. It recognizes over 45 bit-mapped graphics and animation formats and writes over 40 different cross-platform formats. Its color reduction, scaling, and palette manipulating tools are arguably better than Photoshop's. And the Background Removal function, which substitutes a single color for a range of colors, is very useful for creating multimedia titles.

Cross-Platform Palettes

If you plan to show your work across different platforms, you need to be aware that different computer systems use different color palettes to define and limit the infinite number of color combinations that exist. For example, the Macintosh System palette has white in the first position, and black in the last position of the palette. Windows requires that black be first and white be last and as well requires a specific arrangement and color value for the first 10 and last 2 positions of the color palette.

Again, there is software such as DeBabelizer that will help you create a palette that works with different systems.

Changing the Frame and Pixel Aspect

You also need to be aware that different display systems use different frame and pixel aspect ratios. A Macintosh display and an NTSC television, for example, both employ a 4:3 frame ratio. However, some NTSC pixels are rectangular at a resolution of 720×486 pixels, while a Macintosh creates and uses square pixels. If you display one on the other, shapes and motion are distorted and appear stretched. To convert one into the other, use programs such as Adobe's After Effects to reconcile the differences.

IH025615.JPG IH026679.JPG IH026716.JPG IH026701.JPG

IH026717.JPG ih069808.JPG mb009070.JPG RT001336.JPG

AL012134.JPG mb009020.JPG mb007742.JPG mb009135.JPG

mb009220.JPG mb009099.JPG IH031241.JPG RT001595.JPG

na006995.JPG na006994.JPG na006993.JPG na006989.JPG

Chapter 6

Organizing and Managing Images

If your new media project uses more than a few dozen images, or if you obtained images from many sources, you must be particularly well organized. You'll need a viable system for logging and tracking valuable content as it moves through the various stages of your project and special software to help catalog and organize the images after they are in digital form. You'll also need enough storage space to hold all your digital data. If you aren't well organized, the consequences range from annoying delays to shocking charges from sources for lost content.

NOTE   If your project consists of only a few dozen self-created images, managing and organizing them is important, but not complicated. The digital files can be titled with a simple verbal descriptor and placed in a folder residing on an internal or external hard drive. Be sure to create a duplicate file of all your images and store it safely elsewhere.

Logging and Tracking Original Art

It's critical that you keep track of images as they come in the door—or arrive digitally from cyberspace. To do this, you need to create a picture log. This log should include the following information:

Before you Begin   Acquiring the Image   **Preparing the Image**   Using the Image   Showing the Image

▶ Source of the images

▶ Date you received the images

▶ Number of images

▶ Type description of each image (for example, color, black-and-white, slides, prints, or digital file)

▶ Log in number

▶ Name of the person who actually received the image

In general, it is best to keep the images in one central location until a selection is made and a digital copy is created. If the images are going to be passed around the office or studio, however, you'll want to keep track of where they are using the log. This applies primarily to precious analog images rather than digital files, which can be easily duplicated. When the image is returned to the source, this should be noted in the log.

The log can be a simple handwritten piece of paper, or a database or spreadsheet program. It's not a bad idea to have both an electronic log and a handwritten version, in case one is lost or destroyed.

Handling Images

The minute an image comes in the door, you are responsible for it. If it is an original slide or print and it is lost or damaged, costs can be as high as $2,000 per image. Keep the slides and prints away from heat or liquids. Slides are very sensitive to bright light and can begin fading in just a few hours. Keep them in protective packaging at all times and only remove the protection when you are ready to digitize the image. When handling vintage prints or original slides use lint-free cotton gloves, which will keep damaging acids and oils on your fingers from corrupting the surface.

When you receive a digital file—either on a SyQuest-type cartridge or on a CD-ROM—immediately make a backup. Carefully store the original media or return it to the sender. If you lose a custom-created CD, you may be liable for replacing it at a cost of several hundred dollars.

Imagebases

It can be quite a task to store and catalog prints, slides, and other tangible content. It can be even more difficult when the image is stored on a computer's hard drive in digital form. As a digital file, the image might exist only in a directory or in a folder with a cryptic reference number or a short title. At best, the image might be represented by a small thumbnail image on the screen. Finding one specific image in a directory that contains hundreds, if not thousands, of images can be like finding a needle in a haystack.

Software such as Adobe's Fetch, Canto's Cumulus, and DCI's ImageAXS exist to make the job of organizing digital images easier. These imagebases, as they are sometimes called to differentiate them from more traditional data-bases, usually consist of a database, a search function, and a viewer. They are compatible with most image file formats. They commonly organize images both textually and visually. The text portion of these programs operates much like any database by entering key descriptors into a field. Typically these descriptors include a variety of pertinent data, including the source of the image, the date the image was made or acquired, a reference number, and a verbal description of the image itself. The verbal description can be literal or figurative. In other words, you might describe an image as "Red Car on Hollywood Blvd," or figuratively, as "Leisure, Fun, Sexy." Like any database, its usefulness is determined by how you organize your fields and the words you choose. Textual search methods vary from software to software. Some use the simple flat file search methods, which literally look for a single word or combinations of letters, while other programs use the more flexible and precise Boolean method, which uses the qualifiers "and," "or," and "not."

Another common component of imagebases is a lightbox, which attempts to imitate the familiar look and feel of an actual lightbox used by professional picture editors to sort and edit images. A thumbnail version of the image appears on the screen, and at quick glance you can find what you are looking for. Images you select can then be placed in a separate lightbox you have created for that purpose. To see a thumbnail image in a higher resolution, you can click on it and a larger version of the picture will fill your monitor screen.

Figure 6.1   A typical imagebase.

Returning Images

When an analog image or digital medium is returned, it should be sent via FedEx, UPS Overnight, Airborne, or an overnight service that provides a detailed log of the status of the shipment. U.S. Postal Certified Mail is okay, but it's not considered the safest way to return material. For most commercial carriers, the value of an image is considered to be the value of the film or cartridge itself and *not* the value attached to the actual content. Because there is a huge gap between the material cost and the content value, you might want to consider additional insurance on top of what is provided by the carrier.

Packaging should be secure, with slides inside slide sheets and protected by cardboard, prints carefully sandwiched between two sheets of stiff cardboard, and digital media, such as SyQuest cartridges, wrapped in bubble wrap. Label the outside of the package "Photos (or Images): Handle with Care. Do not Bend." For digital media, label the package "Magnetic Material: Avoid Exposure to All Magnetic Fields." Include in the package a memo describing the contents. You also might want to include a self-addressed stamped envelope, with a note to be signed by the receiver and returned acknowledging receipt in good order of the material.

Digital Storage

At this time there is no single solution for storing large amounts of digital image data. Instead, it is common to use a variety of storage devices, sometimes alone, but more often in combination with each other. The most typical storage options are as follows:

- ▶ Hard drives, internal or external

- ▶ Removable cartridges with SyQuest-type drives that hold anywhere from 44 MB to 1 GB of digital data

- ▶ Digital Audio Tape (DAT) players that store computer data on cassettes

- ▶ Writeable CD players that "burn" data onto discs that hold up to 660 MB of data and are compatible with almost any CD-ROM player

Each of these systems has its advantages and disadvantages.

Hard Drives

Hard drives, including those that come with most personal computers, are fast—data is quickly read and written—and also economical. Gigabyte hard drives, for example, which hold 1,000 screen resolution images, often go for under $500. However, hard drives store only a finite amount of data and fill up quickly. They are bulky and relatively fragile, and therefore not easily transported. They are best suited for use in the actual process of working with images, rather than as a long-term storage device.

Removable Cartridge Drives

Removable cartridge drives, such as the SyQuest and Bernoulli drives, are slower than most hard drives. What they lack in speed, they make up in convenience. Cartridges capable of holding hundreds of megabytes of data are inserted like floppy disks into a drive mechanism. When they are full, they can be removed and replaced by another, low-cost cartridge. Once removed from the player, the cartridge can be sent anywhere in the world (assuming, of course, that someone on the receiving end has a compatible player). Increasingly popular are the Zip and EZ drives, which hold 100 MB and 135 MB respectively. (The newest Zip drive supports 1 GB cartridges.) These new, low-cost drives use small, very inexpensive cartridges. Because the drives are so small, they can be carried anywhere you go—or conceivably sent along with a cartridge to someone who needs the data but doesn't personally own a drive. Like their bigger cousins, these small drives suffer a major limitation: incompatibility. To read an EZ cartridge, for example, you need an EZ drive. Other SyQuest drives won't work. And of course EZ cartridges are not compatible with Zip drives, which are made by a competitor.

DAT Tape

For economical storage nothing beats DAT tape. DAT players cost less than $500, and a cassette that holds around 4 GB of data costs only $15. The problem is that DAT storage systems are very slow due to design. Data is transferred linearly onto the tape, so if the image you want is on the opposite end of the tape from where you currently are, you must wait as the drive advances the tape to that spot. Compatibility between systems is not always assured.

Keep in mind that all of the storage solutions mentioned here—hard drives, removable cartridges, and DAT—share a major limitation. Because they employ some type of magnetic read/write technology, over time they are susceptible to data loss. In fact, depending on circumstances, data can become corrupted in just a few years. And if the medium is exposed to a heavy dosage of X-rays—which might occur if a drive, cartridge, or tape is mailed or shipped abroad—the data can be instantly erased.

CD Writeable

This brings us to CD Writeable, which is perhaps the most versatile storage and distribution solution for a multimedia producer. Not only are the discs that these devices write to stable—tests show they safely store data for over 20 years—but the discs are compatible with just about any common CD-ROM player, a standard feature of most computers sold today. In the past, the barrier to using devices that can both write to and read data from a CD was primarily economical. However, prices for CD Writeable devices continue to plummet, and they are available for under $1,000. The discs cost only about $10 for 660 MB of unformatted data. (Note that there are CD Writeable devices that cost less than $500, but require the use of more expensive— $50—discs.) CDs are easy to store, ship, and use, and are impervious to X-rays.

NOTE   Think of slides and prints as cost-effective storage. (A single 35mm color slide, for example, contains hundreds of megabytes of information.) Keep an analog version of the image handy and scan at the desired resolution when needed.

Compression

Some sort of image compression is important at every stage of a project's development, from sending and receiving images online, to storing images economically and saving valuable storage space.

What exactly is compression? The technique is not unlike the manufacture of apple juice that is condensed for shipping at a plant and reconstituted at home. Compression algorithms have been developed that reduce all the numbers in the image file to more efficient equations representing the entire image file. Thus the compressed images are packaged for more convenient transfer and then, once received, are decompressed to their original size allowing them to be displayed or printed.

Just as reconstituted apple juice will not be identical to fresh juice, compressed images can suffer the same fate. The objective is always to remove only that information from the image that can be reconstructed at the receiving end with no noticeable degradation.

There are basically two compression techniques for saving data: lossy and lossless. *Lossy* is the most efficient compression technique, but it requires discarding certain data that may or may not affect the overall quality of the image. Ratios of 100:1 are possible using lossy techniques. *Lossless* means just that. By ridding the picture of redundant information, the image is compressed, but nothing significant is lost. Ratios of 2:1 are about the best you can do using lossless techniques.

An example of lossy compression is JPEG. The Joint Photographic Experts Group (JPEG) came up with a method designed to achieve the highest quality compression by removing redundant data and data to which the human eye is less sensitive. The actual amount of compression achievable is dependent on the software you use, the compression setting you choose, and the image content. Photoshop, for example, offers four settings, low, medium, high, and maximum, while other utilities such as Image Alchemy or ProJPEG offer more options for control. Simple images with few details and wide expanses of similar colors will compress more than complex images with lots of details and frequent color gradations. In all cases, the more compression you apply, the smaller the file, but the more lost detail. Because JPEG is an international standard for compressing still images, JPEG compressed files can easily be opened by most imaging software.

Examples of lossless compression include the popular software programs StuffIt Deluxe, DiskDoubler, Norton Utilities, and Compact Pro (for the Mac), plus PKZIP and ZipIt for the PC. GIF is also a lossless compression technique that only works on indexed color images (8 bit or less), which limits you to using 256 colors at best. Kodak's proprietary Photo CD process (YCC) is also a lossless compression technique that uses complex algorithms to decompress. (That's why it takes so long to open a high-resolution Photo CD file.)

As with lossy compression, lossless works better with simple images rather than complex, detailed ones. As a general rule of thumb, use lossless compression techniques for image storage and lossy compression such as JPEG for transferring images across cyberspace. For images destined to a Web site, GIF is often used despite being a lossless, and therefore less efficient, compression technique. At this time GIF is the only fully supported format that allows you to create both transparent and interlaced pixels. (More on this in Chapter 9, "Still Images on the Web.")

Remember that it takes special software to compress files and special software to decompress the files. If you are sending files to someone else, make sure he or she has the necessary software to decompress your file. If you are receiving a compressed file, be sure you have the capacity to decompress it. Many compression programs give you the option of creating a self-extracting archive (.sea), which makes it possible to open a file regardless of what software you have available. Image editing programs, such as Photoshop or DeBabilizer, can read most compressed files. To read a file created using StuffIt, however, requires UnstuffIt, a program that is widely available on the Internet as shareware and as a commercial product.

NOTE   Every time you compress an image using lossy techniques, the image quality is decreased. It is wise to compress only when you have completed your image editing and processing and are ready to either transmit or store the image.

NOTE   If an image is already compressed (regardless of the technique), other compression techniques can do nothing to reduce the image size. In fact, with disk-doubling software such as StuffIt, trying to compress already compressed image files sometimes makes the file larger rather than smaller in size.

Keep in mind, as you patiently wait for an image to appear on your Web page or to download from an image provider, that image compression techniques continue to improve. Companies, driven by the market for products that make it possible to move images more quickly across limited bandwidth and store huge qualities of images on finite storage space, are experimenting with more sophisticated compression techniques that offer higher compression ratios with less trade-offs. In particular, look for new products that use wavelet and fractal compression techniques, which today look very promising.

NOTE   File size is determined by the number of pixels that make up an image and the number of bits it takes to describe each pixel. (1 bit for black-and-white, 8 bits for 256 colors or shades of gray, 24 bits for RGB color, and so on.) A typical, uncompressed, 640×480 24-bit screen resolution image takes up 900K of data space on a storage medium.

Case Study:

Corbis on the Process of Organizing Images
A discussion with Corbis' Lisa Anderson, producer.

After we have negotiated with an image provider for the images—sometimes this is a lengthy process—and have come to an understanding over price and use, we still have to actually receive the image. We then might spend up to another two months reminding or assisting our source to send the images to use for use in the product; we try to take this potential delay into our product sched-

ule. When we finally receive the images, they are rarely in digital form. The images come to us as black-and-white prints, 35mm or 4"×5" transparencies, or in the case of some museums, paintings, or 8"×10" transparencies. Still, we don't take the images when they arrive and start working with them immediately—even though sometimes we are anxious to do so.

continues

Case Study, continued

After the images come in, they are formally trafficked. This is really important, especially when you are dealing with stock agencies who often include agreements that state that if you damage a slide you owe them $2,000 or more (simply by accepting the package, you've agreed to these contract conditions) or with one-of-a-kind original documents and vintage photographs that can't be replaced. Only once the photographs and slides have been logged in using bar code numbers are the pictures allowed to come to me.

Then the producer, research assistants, and designers carefully review the material for potential use. For example, we look at groups of slides and transparencies on a light table. We edit vintage photography and unsleeved negatives wearing archival gloves. The images that we choose are assigned unique tracking numbers. Information about the source, when the images came in and in some cases when they are due to return, and contractual use restrictions are all logged into a database created for the product. The producers work closely with the intellectual property specialists on our staff who assist us in clearing all rights including underlying rights associated with any of the material—images, music, and so forth—we use in the products; they also assist us in drawing up use agreements with our sources. We follow the straight and narrow in setting up and maintaining traffic and intellectual property processes. We are very careful to follow the guidelines about use, cropping, and so on, mandated by the source of the images.

Part III

Using the Image

na006975.JPG na006972.JPG na006920.JPG na006925.JPG

na006918.JPG na006914.JPG na005646.JPG na005664.JPG

na005641.JPG IH027207.JPG IH027198.JPG IH027211.JPG

IH027217.JPG IH027221.JPG IH027227.JPG IH027230.JPG

IH027249.JPG IH026900.JPG IH026914.JPG IH026891.JPG

Chapter 7

The Electronic Canvas: Design and Software Tools for the New Media

Part I looked at how to find or make the images you need. Part II addressed how to prepare those images for electronic display. In theory then, the digital images—with some fine tuning—are ready to be incorporated into your new media project.

There are many ways that your still images can be used. They can appear on the screen alone, as part of a sequence, or in combination with other media such as sound, text, and animation. What you eventually decide to do will depend on several considerations.

The first and foremost consideration is the message you are trying to convey and the scope of your project. This takes you back to the section at the beginning of the book, "Before You Begin," when you were deciding who your audience was, the type of your presentation, what your message was, and the size of your budget. Say, for example, you are giving a presentation on a somber and serious subject—you might not want your accompanying visuals to overwhelm, but rather only to accent or inspire a mood. On the other hand, if you are trying to entertain, you might be interested in flashy techniques that draw attention to the project itself.

Whatever you try to do—motivate, educate, or entertain—you'll need to apply a combination of graphic design techniques and authoring software to realize your vision. Graphic design establishes the relationship between the image and the other elements of the project. If done properly, design intensifies the message and gives your project a special resonance that will draw in or challenge your audience. Authoring or presentation software, such as Macromedia Director and Adobe Persuasion, is the glue that holds everything together. Authoring and presentation software vary widely, so you'll need to know which software package is appropriate for your project.

In the next chapter, specific uses of still images ranging from a single image on a screen to a complex multimedia extravaganza are discussed. Design and tools for the Web, which has its own set of issues, are discussed in the last chapter. To begin, here are some basic graphic design considerations that apply to all new media projects that rely on still images, as well as an overview of some of the more commonly available software tools that will help you get your message across.

Design for the Electronic Canvas and the New Media

Design for the new media is new. At this time, very few people have been trained exclusively to design for the new media. Instead, most people who are producing or designing for the new media come from the traditional media, such as graphic artists, writers, TV producers, film makers, illustrators, and photographers.

It's understandable then that each designer brings his or her own perspective and way of doing things when designing a multimedia project. For example, a graphic designer might feel right at home laying out a screen that includes type and other graphics elements such as borders, lines, and frames—and yet feel awkward using sound and animation, or creating transitions between screens. Writers will naturally fill the screen with text and might use images timidly. Some photographers will be hesitant to manipulate and alter their images, being more comfortable putting so-called straight photographs on the screen. Film and TV people might be very confident using sound and animation and sequenced narratives, but not so sure of the best use of text. And so on.

Case Study:
Doug Rowan/CEO Corbis

Rowan is the president and chief executive officer for Corbis. Previously, he was the president of AXS (now DCI, Inc.). Rowan is in charge of the Corbis and Bettmann image licensing group and Corbis Publishing. Image licensing provides content from the vast Corbis digital archive—some of which you can see here in this book and on the accompanying CD-ROM. Corbis Publishing produced and published such award-winning documentaries as "A Passion for Art," "Volcanoes: Life on the Edge," and "Critical Mass: America's Race to Build the Atomic Bomb." Corbis was founded in 1989 by Bill Gates to create new uses and markets for digital content.

Rowan on the difference between books and multimedia

I love books, but book models should not be used in the CD-ROM publishing world. After all, what is a book? It is sequential. It has a table of contents, an index, and chapters. Navigation tends to be front-to-back linear. At Corbis, when we discuss CD-ROM titles, we always ask ourselves: what can we do for the electronic canvas that you can't do in a book? For example, we can create contextual links that connect words with other words, or links that connect words with images. And then, of course, there is sound. I don't want a photographic title to exist without audio, ever. The audio could be the roar of a lion, or music, or a voice-over. Besides sound, I want the image to be interactive. I want a viewer to be able to explore an image. Take, for example, a family photograph. It could be looked at many ways. The viewer could enlarge the image and examine facial expressions and features of individuals closely. Links could be created that provide a contextual depth to each person. Other links could connect a viewer to outtakes from the same shoot, giving an entirely new dimension to the original image.

The reality is that multimedia is evolving, and the boundaries between different media are blurring. We are all learning from each other, picking the best from each discipline. (Sometimes it seems like we are picking the worst—but that is another story!) What are today's truths in multimedia design may well become tomorrow's clichés.

Having said all this, there are still some givens that apply to design for new media, such as design basics, which should always be taken into account. The electronic canvas, for example, is not a cave wall, nor a piece of papyrus, nor a piece of high–gloss book paper. While it shares some characteristics with its older cousins, it has its own advantages and disadvantages (as listed here) that must be clearly understood by anyone wishing to design for it.

▶ The electronic canvas is usually horizontal, which means full-frame vertical images will be cropped or reduced.

▶ Creating color for the electronic canvas means understanding the additive process (adding Red, Green, and Blue light to Black) rather than the subtractive process used in traditional printing, which starts with white paper and then subtracts color through the use of Cyan, Magenta, and Yellow pigments.

▶ Monitors that use CRT technology inherently flicker—some more than others—and therefore reading lots of text off a CRT monitor is not something most people enjoy.

▶ Because monitors require a power source, they are not cuddly or bath-friendly like books. This is something to consider when contemplating the context in which your work will be seen. People who climb into bed with their laptops to read a romance story are rare, but in the future when "intimate" full-color, high-resolution, battery-operated LCD screens become more common, this might change.

▶ Not all display systems are the same, and you have little control over how your work actually appears on other people's systems. Also, the speed in which images come up on the screen is dependent on the specifications of the user's CPU and graphics card. Resolution is mostly limited to 72 or 96 dpi. (On the other hand, you don't have to budget for expensive paper, or worry about images fading or yellowing with time as one does in traditional design work.)

Because of these considerations you might want to do the following:

▶ Limit the use of complementary colors—red and green, blue and orange, purple and yellow—especially when it come to text on a background. These color combinations will appear to vibrate and will enhance the flickering effect of some monitors. (Of course, there are times when you may want this effect.)

▶ Stay away from huge blocks of text. Few people like to read from a screen.

▶ Avoid graphics and images with lots of detail.

▶ Understand that television dominates our experience with the electronic canvas—and creates certain expectations as a result. For example, people generally expect at least something to move on a monitor. They also expect to hear sound.

As with any traditional design project—be it for print or screen—design remains a process of combining basic components, including text, type, graphics elements such as borders, patterns, lines, and colors, and the still image in a way that doesn't interfere with the transfer of the desired content. Whether you work in a group or alone, the process you follow to achieve this is straightforward. Follow these steps:

1. Start with a brainstorming session and verbalize a concept based on the audience and your message. Use words that relate to what you want to convey, words such as fun, new, sexy, racy, soft, elegant, mature, and so forth.

2. Next create comps or rough sketches, using pencil and paper, that turn the verbal into a visual map or script. A low-tech approach is desirable because there are no computer crashes or incompatible software to interfere with the free flow of ideas. To do this, apply your verbal concepts to the various graphic and textual elements that you wish to include. For example, should the text be funky or traditional? Should the color be bright and neon or deep and rich? One choice will evoke fun and lightheartedness, the other formality and seriousness. Apply this verbal game to the images themselves as well. In all cases, when choosing the images, use the strongest ones. Avoid weak images and when in doubt leave that image out. Make a photocopy of each image you choose. Place them together to see how they connect.

3. Play with contrast by juxtapositioning opposites to create a different effect. Keep in mind a goal of stylistic unity, not necessarily uniformity. Try to create a harmonious environment where a variety of different elements can coexist. Your map or script should now show where the different elements go and how they interact with each other.

4. Set up a system for getting feedback, and then apply revisions and adjustments.

5. Zero in on a single concept that works, then fine-tune it. Be prepared to spend lots of time on revisions and, at the same time, adhere as much as possible to a realistic schedule.

6. Using authoring or presentation software, pull your ideas together into a single cohesive project.

Detailed design techniques and theory are beyond the scope of this book, but I suggest you look at the work of others to better understand what works and what doesn't. Examples of good design for the electronic canvas abound, although bad examples do as well. On the accompanying CD-ROM are excerpts from a few projects that I think have successfully used still images and smart design to great effect. Professional graphic design organizations and magazines, such as *Communications Arts*, hold annual new media design contests and publish the winners on CD-ROMs, which can be a great source for inspiration and ideas.

Miscellaneous Design Techniques

Here are a few tips and techniques for creating your own backgrounds, drop shadows, and frames. These design techniques will come in handy for almost any multimedia project that uses still images.

Creating Backgrounds

Both realistic and abstract images can be used as backgrounds in your multimedia projects. Properly used, a background can reinforce the graphics elements that overlay it. If used incorrectly, a background can dominate and interfere with the primary message you want to convey. Most successful backgrounds are low contrast and contain muted colors that complement the foreground images or text. Backgrounds can be purchased as clip art from a variety of sources, or you can create them yourself. On the accompanying CD-ROM, we've carefully selected some images for their potential as backgrounds. They are royalty-free, meaning we retain the copyright to the images themselves, but you can use them any way you wish in your multimedia projects. (The Corbis Images on the accompanying CD-ROM, however, are not royalty free. They are for your personal use only. If you want to use them for any other purpose, you will first need to contact the company directly.)

NOTE   Before you make your own backgrounds from any other images be sure
         you have the rights to use the image.

Using Photoshop to Create a Backdrop

Simply adjust the tonal values of the image by using brightness/contrast,
levels, or curves tools. Create several variations to choose from. Use filters
such as "emboss" for special effects. Resize the image to the appropriate
dimensions.

Drop shadows often are added to still images to add depth to an otherwise
two-dimensional scene. They are easily created.

Using Photoshop to Create a Drop Shadow

Open your image file. Open the Layers window (Window:Palettes:Show
Layers). Change the background to a layer by double-clicking on it. Rename
this layer "Image." Increase the size of your canvas by approximately 1" in
both the vertical and horizontal directions (Image:Canvas Size). Select the
entire image and create a new layer and call it "Shadow." Select the new layer
and then feather it 10–15 pixels (Select: Feather). Fill the selection with 35
percent black (Edit:Fill). Move the selection filled with gray in the direction
you want the shadow to fall. Move the shadow layer below the image layer,
and then merge the layers.

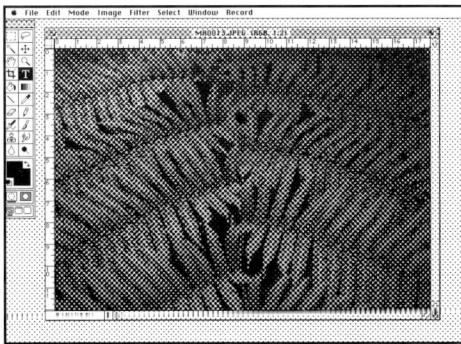

Figure 7.1 Creating drop shadows.

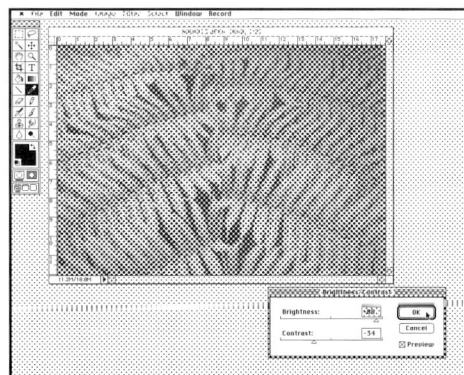

Figure 7.2 Creating drop shadows.

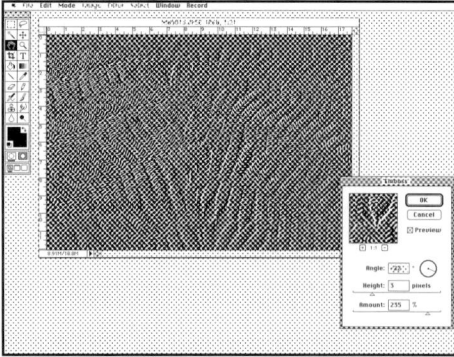

Figure 7.3 Creating drops shadows.

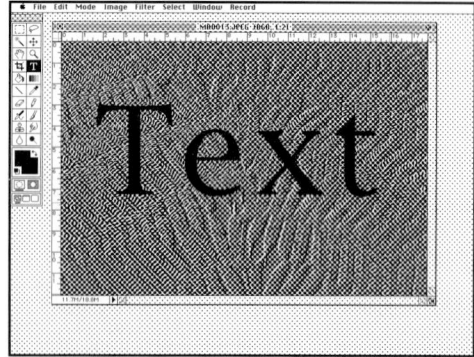

Figure 7.4 Creating drop shadows.

Creating Frames

Frames are another way of adding dimensionally to a still image. Ready-made digital frames can be purchased as clip art, but there are many ways frames can be made using Photoshop. One simple method is to select the image, and then under the Select menu choose Modify: Border. Type in 20–50 pixels (or wider). Now use a Fill Command (Edit: Fill) or filter the selection. (You may want to enlarge your canvas to give you more room around the edge of the image.

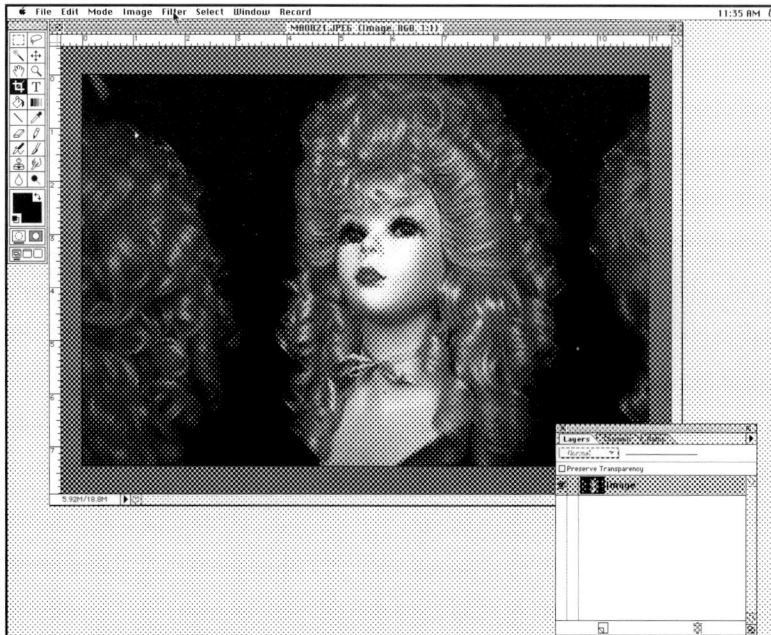

Figure 7.5 Creating frames.

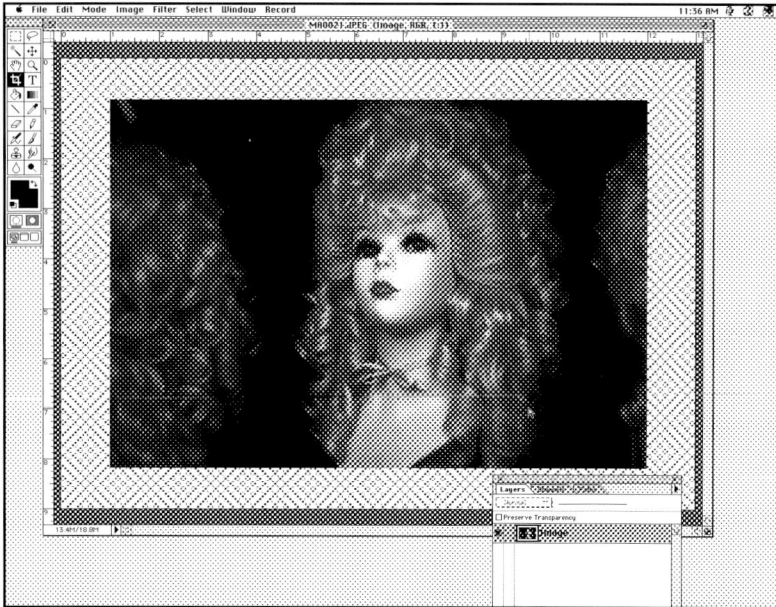

Figure 7.6 Creating frames.

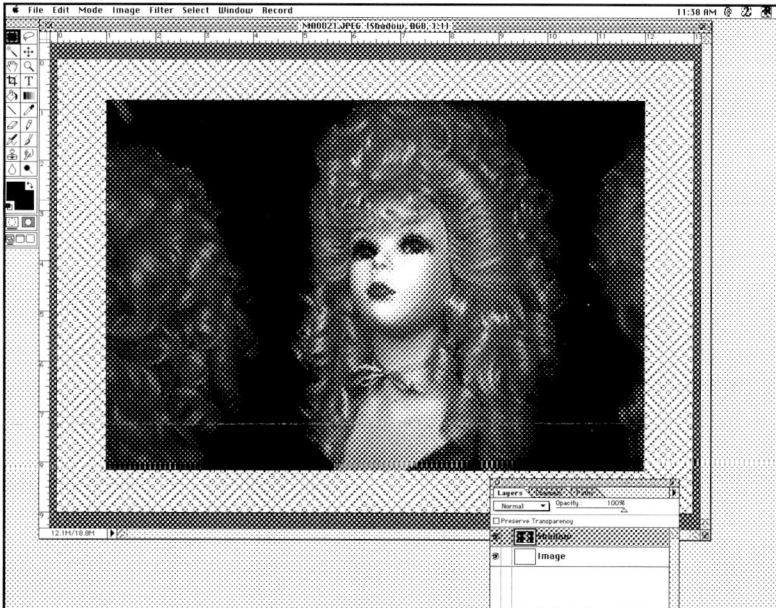

Figure 7.7 Creating frames.

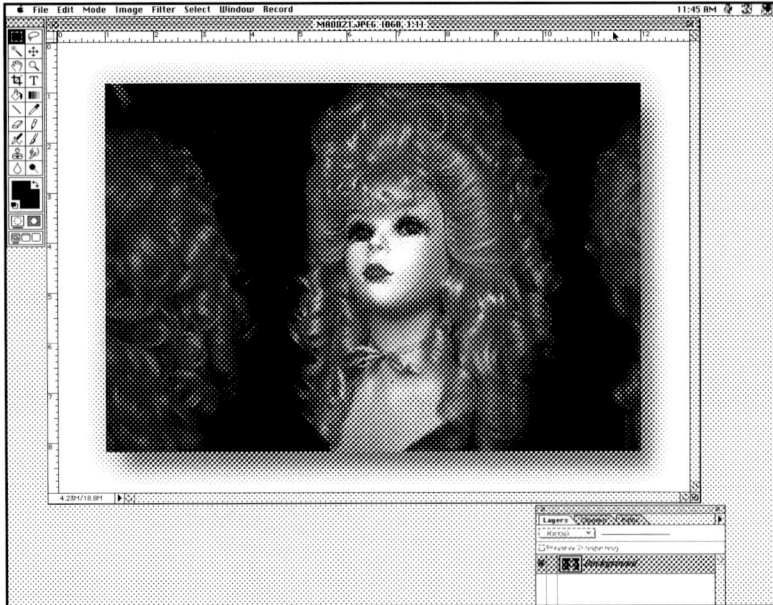

Figure 7.8   Creating frames.

Software Authoring Tools

Are you giving a presentation to a group and want to include digital images with some text and graphs? Are you just interested in displaying a sequence of still images for, say, a portfolio presentation? Are you interested in authoring a fully developed multimedia project, one that might eventually be published on a CD-ROM and sold commercially?

Each of these projects can require different multimedia authoring software. What you choose will depend on your budget and your approach. Authoring software is available in a wide range of price, flexibility, and ease-of-use.

On the accompanying CD-ROM, you'll actually find trial versions of some of the more popular commercial multimedia authoring programs to test out for yourself. In the appendix you'll find addresses and phone numbers for ordering the other software mentioned in the next section. (If none of the commercial products are appropriate for you, there is always the option of creating your own—but if you can do that it means you really know what you are doing and you probably don't need to be reading this section!)

Presentation Software

The software listed here is meant specifically for developing and designing presentations. Templates often are provided with the software to make it as easy as possible to integrate digital images with a page of text or graphs. The software usually ranges in price from $150-$300.

▶ Adobe Persuasion. Persuasion provides a complete set of tools, including outlining, word processing, drawing, charting, and formatting, to combine text and graphics with images to create multimedia presentations. It comes with built-in transitional effects, templates, and background textures, and several easy-to-read typefaces to choose from. Macintosh and Windows versions are both available. A new release is expected soon that will make it a snap to put presentations up on the Web.

▶ Microsoft PowerPoint. PowerPoint is bundled with Microsoft's Office, so the installed base for this program is huge. Because this program is so popular, there is a lot of support for it, especially online via the Web. PowerPoint presentations are cross-platform, so they can be opened on both Macintosh or Windows computers. The program comes with lots of templates.

▶ Gold Disk Astound. Astound is a very easy program to learn. It takes no time to create dynamic presentations complete with images, sound, and animation. Special effects such as spinning, bouncing, and rotating can be easily added to any object. The program can import both Persuasion and PowerPoint files. Drawing tools are included, but they are not as extensive as those found in Persuasion and PowerPoint.

▶ Kodak's Arrange-It. Arrange-It enables you to build and display interactive presentations using Photo CD images, as well as images in the TIFF or PICT formats, and sound files. Once complete, a file is sent to a Kodak Photo CD Portfolio service provider and a Kodak Portfolio CD is created. This disc can then be viewed on a television using a Kodak Photo CD player or on a computer.

Simple Image Sequencing

There are inexpensive products ($100 and less) available that enable you to simply present a sequence of still images—as a portfolio or for use at a kiosk or a trade booth. They offer limited text and sound support and only basic interactivity, such as stop and start commands.

NOTE   Some of the imagebases mentioned in Chapter 6—Adobe's Fetch, Canto's Cumulus, and DCI's ImageAXS—also have the capacity to sequence still images into a self-running "slide show." Images on a Kodak Photo CD also can be played sequentially using a Kodak Photo CD player and a television, or on a computer with software that comes with each Photo CD.

▶ QuickShow. QuickShow from MetaTools is a simple program that you drop into a folder of PICT files (as many as you want), and when you double-click on the application, it brings each of the images in the folder up in a repeating slide show. It is simple, yet very effective and easy to use.

▶ Museum. Museum is shareware for the Macintosh created by Rustle Laidman that imports PICT and JPEG files and text and .snd sound files and creates a self-running or controlled slide show. (Suggested price $5.)

▶ ZedCard. ZedCard is an add-on to DCI's ImageAXS software, and it organizes and displays up to nine high-quality images with captions on a single floppy disk. ZedCard can be used as an electronic portfolio, providing a cost-effective alternative to supplying books of photo-graphic prints or tear sheets to clients.

Fully Developed Interactive Multimedia Projects

Annual reports, training programs, advertising collateral, entertainment, scholarly projects, games, and other CD-ROM–based commercial products call for more feature-laden multimedia authoring tools. Most of these advanced (and often more expensive) tools also can be used to create presen-tations or simple image sequences.

Keep in mind that if you are planning to make a commercial project by using one of these programs and subsequently distributing it, you have to factor in the licensing costs. (Another advantage of works built around custom-made software is there are no licensing fees to worry about.)

NOTE   Programs such as Director are multiplatform, which means theoretically they can be run on both the Macintosh or PC. The reality, however, is cross-platform programs don't always work so well because fonts, color palettes, or color depth are handled differently by different platforms. For this reason, many producers choose to develop for only one or the other platform, or make two different versions, each optimized for one specific platform.

▶ Macromedia Director. Director is one of the most popular and powerful off-the-shelf multimedia authoring tools, available for both Windows and Macintosh (commonly available for around $800). It features 48 layers of independent movable objects called sprites, as well as simultaneous sound effects from two sound tracks. Interactivity and other special effects can be added by using Lingo, an easy-to-learn, proprietary scripting language. Director can be used to create corporate presentations, entertainment, educational CD-ROMs, digital publications, software demonstrations, and much more. It is a time-based tool, which means that objects such as images, text, and sound and desired effects are laid out next to each other in a linear fashion using a "score" that looks and acts like a common spreadsheet.

▶ Authorware Professional. Authorware Professional is best used for large projects that incorporate lots of graphics and textual elements and require a high-level of interactive control. It is visually-based, meaning users can build applications without scripting. The program is available for both Windows and the Macintosh. Retail cost is around $5,000.

▶ Apple Media Kit. Apple Media Kit consists of the Apple Media Tool (list $495) and the Apple Media Programming Environment (list $995). (Purchased together they cost $1,100.) The Tool uses a very simple visual interface and is designed for people who don't have programming skills. The Environment adds sophisticated interactive capabilities and is meant to be used by those people with Pascal or C programming language experience. Products developed using this kit use QuickTime to play back on both PCs with Windows and Macintosh computers.

The latest version of the Apple Media Tool (v.2.0) supports Apple QuickTime VR.

▶ mTropolis. mTropolis is a high end authoring system (list price $4,995) based on object-oriented programming. This means that you don't need to know a scripting language to build in interactivity. Instead, visual icons are drag-and-dropped into place. This method is much different from Director's linear score-and-cast method and the stack orientation of HyperCard, SuperCard, and ToolBox. It's not easy to use this program, but once mastered it offers many more features and flexibility than other off-the-shelf authoring tools. It is fast becoming a popular program among serious multimedia producers.

▶ Claris HyperCard. This venerable program, which helped kick off the interactive multimedia revolution, remains one of the more popular authoring tools. It uses HyperTalk, an easy-to-use, English-based scripting language to combine and customize text, graphics, music, still images, and animation. It is a card-and-stack–based authoring tool, which means it follows a metaphor similar to that of traditional books— one "page" or card is followed by another. Some of the most popular interactive products were developed using HyperCard, including Myst and Grandma and Me (Broderbrund). It is commonly available for around $99.

▶ SuperCard. SuperCard is a multimedia authoring system very similar to the card-and-stack–based HyperCard but with more features. The program supported color long before HyperCard did. Its latest version supports multiple windows, animation, both bitmap and draw graphics, and sound. SuperTalk, a superset of the original HyperTalk, is the program's scripting language. Like HyperCard, SuperCard has been used to create a wide variety of commercial entertainment software, interactive training materials, kiosks, tutorials, and electronic magazines. It is commonly available for around $400.

▶ ToolBox. ToolBox also is similar to HyperCard, but for Windows. It uses OpenScript, a script similar to HyperTalk. List price is $195.

Although the following software is used primarily for full-motion video editing, still images can be imported into these programs and powerful special effects such as zooms, pans, and elaborate transitions can be applied. Projects created on these video programs can be easily formatted to TV standards and exported to videotape.

▶ Adobe Premiere. Premiere is the most popular desktop video editing program for the Macintosh. Using Premiere, it is easy to combine still images with video, audio, animation, and graphics, as well as apply special effects to the images themselves. Movies created in Premiere can be added to other multimedia projects or used for stand-alone presentations. It is a linear-based program, which means interactivity, such as is found in Director, is not possible. Commonly available for around $500.

▶ Adobe After Effects. After Effects is a high-end digital video editor and special effects generator with more bells and whistles than Premiere. It is designed for broadcast video professionals but has several useful features that multimedia producers will find extremely useful as well. It is available for around $700.

Case Study:
Thomas Walker, GRAF/x

Walker is the president of the New York-based design firm GRAF/x, which specializes in publication, media, and corporate design. Besides working as a designer on the original *Day in the Life* series for Collins Publishers, Walker worked with Rick Smolan on the innovative book/CD-ROM packages "From Alice to Ocean" and "Passage to Vietnam." Walker is currently developing and designing a series of cross-media projects integrating traditional book and magazine publishing with online Web-site development.

Walker:

Because of multimedia, we are seeing a lot more use of photography in general, and I feel the whole language of still imagery is expanding. We are becoming a much more visual, less text-oriented society.

With each new medium the aesthetics change, and that is especially true for multimedia and the Web. For example, if you use a digital camera to create images for your project you don't have to worry about the cost of film. It becomes like shooting for a movie—you shoot a lot and then edit back at the studio. When you edit you aren't looking for one perfect image—you are looking for sequences of images that tell a story.

When I edit pictures for use in multimedia and especially for the Web, I know that people want the biggest bang for the buck. They want information and speed. They will accept much less technical quality as long as an image appears quickly on the screen. For that reason I use custom color palettes a lot. I just used a photograph of the sky and clouds for a Web page and I actually dropped a few more colors than I should have, just to

continues

Case Study, continued

make the image file size smaller so the image would load on the screen quicker. But the effect worked. There isn't much room for subtlety on the Web anyway, and monitors all vary. When we were working on the "Passage to Vietnam" CD-ROM we tested it on a dozen monitors and each one looked different. Now I just make sure that red apples appear red and trees appear green and there is enough tonal separation between the colors so that no matter what colors actually come up on the screen, they feel different.

Multimedia lends itself very well to the photo essay, but not in the traditional print sense. People want the option to explore in detail lots of images and not just a complete all-in-one picture. For that reason, the use of photography in the electronic media has to be multi-dimensional: you have to give people the option of going into the texture and detail of the image itself and then back to the overview, if they want. All the while, you have to provide a context for the images, create a narrative that holds everything together. This means working with the element of time, something that you don't worry about in traditional western photography and art.

Currently, I get a lot of my inspiration from the artists David Hockney and Robert Rauchenberg, especially from their collages. They have created multidimensional works based on still images, and successfully used the passage of time in their pieces. This is very difficult to do and they have done it well.

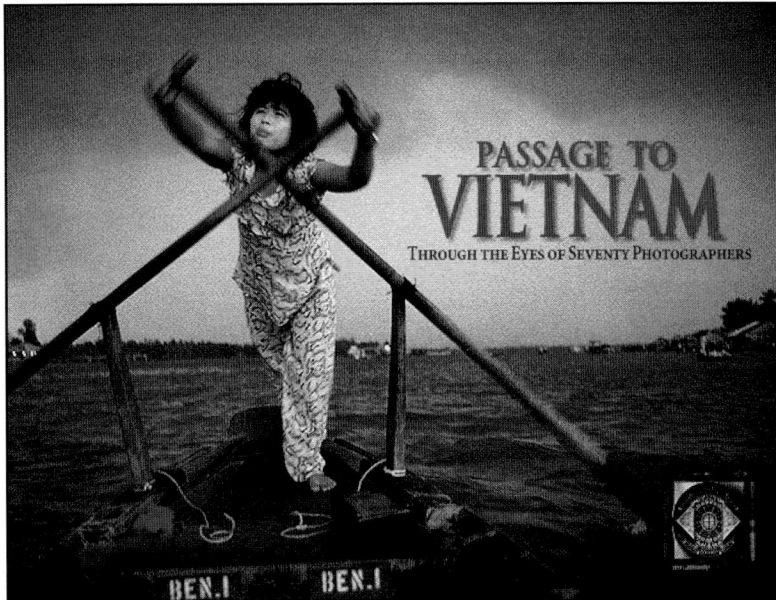

Figure 7.9   An opening screen shot from "A Passage to Vietnam." Produced by Against All Odds and Interval Research in association with Ad-hoc Interactive.

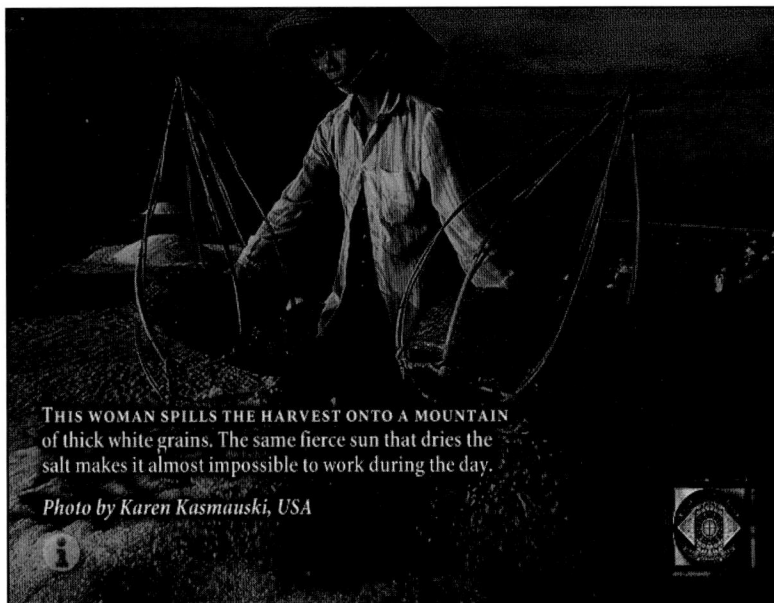

Figure 7.10   A screen shot from "A Passage to Vietnam."

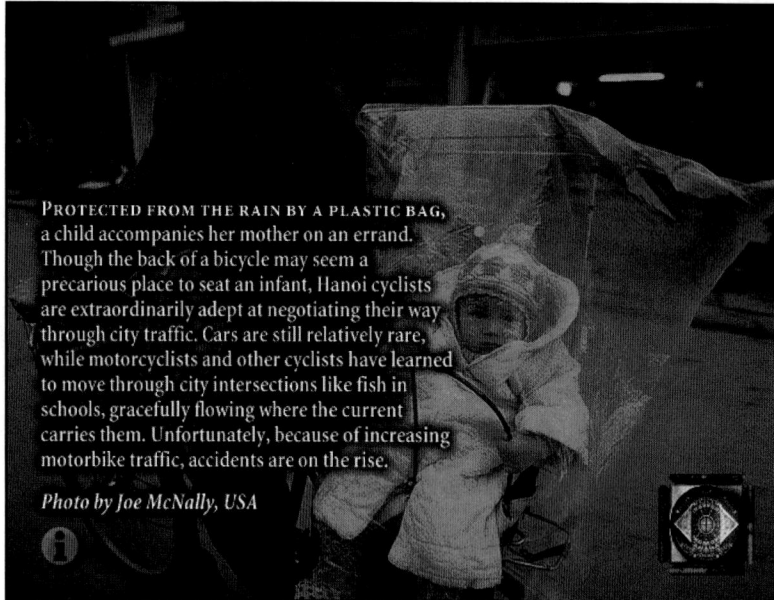

PROTECTED FROM THE RAIN BY A PLASTIC BAG, a child accompanies her mother on an errand. Though the back of a bicycle may seem a precarious place to seat an infant, Hanoi cyclists are extraordinarily adept at negotiating their way through city traffic. Cars are still relatively rare, while motorcyclists and other cyclists have learned to move through city intersections like fish in schools, gracefully flowing where the current carries them. Unfortunately, because of increasing motorbike traffic, accidents are on the rise.

Photo by Joe McNally, USA

Figure 7.11   A screen shot from "A Passage to Vietnam."

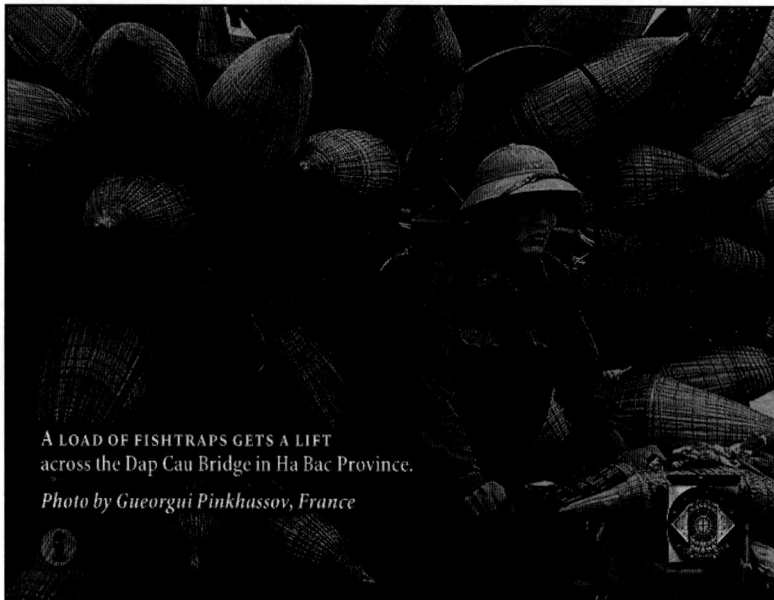

A LOAD OF FISHTRAPS GETS A LIFT across the Dap Cau Bridge in Ha Bac Province.

Photo by Gueorgui Pinkhassov, France

Figure 7.12   A screen shot from "A Passage to Vietnam."

IH026887.JPG
IH026877.JPG
IH026846.JPG
IH026837.JPG
IH026813.JPG
IH026928.JPG
IH026777.JPG
IH026762.JPG
IH026761.JPG
IH026655.JPG
IH026623.JPG
IH026628.JPG
IH026648.JPG
IH026581.JPG
IH026613.JPG
IH026954.JPG
IH027005.JPG
IH027030.JPG
IH027047.JPG
IH027135.JPG

Chapter 8

Combining Images, Text, and Sound

Let's start with the relatively straightforward use of a still image as a simple graphic element on a screen, then work our way through increasing layers of complexity by making still images move, by adding and sequencing other images, adding sound, and finally by creating a virtual reality based on still images.

Remember that it's tempting to want to use the latest three-dimensional effect or slick animation trick just for the sake of a flashy effect. The fact is, no matter how sophisticated your techniques are, after the thrill of the first viewing wears off, you need to ask yourself: Did it work? Did it move the audience to take the action you wanted? Did it educate? Did it inspire? Did the techniques used distract?

Image as Image

A photograph, illustration, or painting can stand alone as the dominant graphic element on the screen—for example as part of an opening page on a Web site—or it can be a component of a larger group of graphic elements or text, for example, a layout of pictures surrounded by text. In either case, there is not much difference between the way a digital image is chosen and used and the way an image or images might be used on a printed page, except for the inherent limitations of the electronic medium.

Before you Begin   Acquiring the Image   Preparing the Image   **Using the Image**   Showing the Image

Keep these things in mind:

▶ Select images for their appropriateness and visual strength.

▶ Show the value you place on an image by the size you choose to present it.

▶ Run highly detailed images in larger sizes.

▶ Crop a weak image to make it look better. (Cropping, however, can ruin a good picture.)

▶ Create tension by using images of varying sizes. Tension keeps the viewer involved and interested, whereas uniformity is boring.

Besides the physical placement of an image on the screen, certain special effects can help make images stand out. (See the illustrations on the next two pages.)

▶ Silhouette an image to eliminate superfluous background details and transform it from the traditional rectangular or square format into something more visually interesting.

▶ Surround an image with a border of varying width depending on the desired effect to highlight and call attention to it.

▶ Use drop shadows to create a three-dimensional effect and emphasize the image or aspects of the image.

▶ Use full-screen bleeds to push the image to the edge and create dynamic tension.

▶ "Shatter," "cube," "slice," or "break" an image apart for a dramatic effect.

(Remember, if you plan to significantly alter an image, make sure you have the rights to do so.)

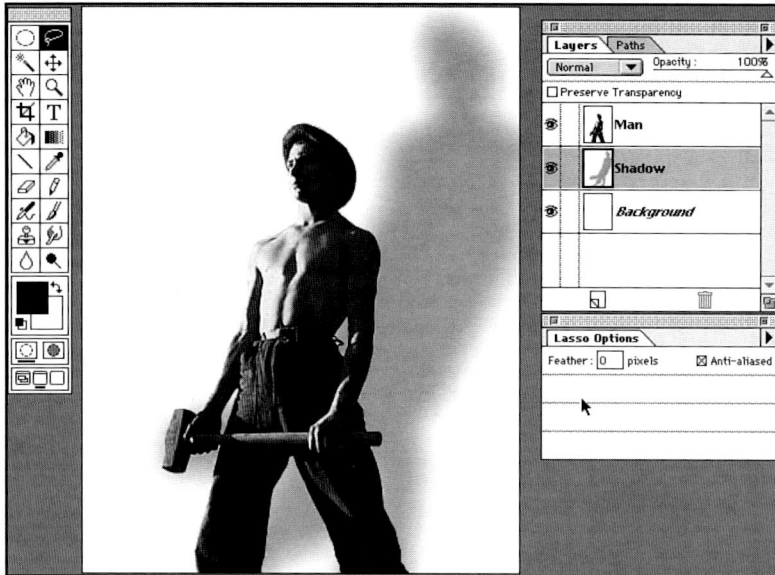

Figure 8.1   Image with a drop shadow.

Figure 8.2   Image that has been shattered, or broken apart.

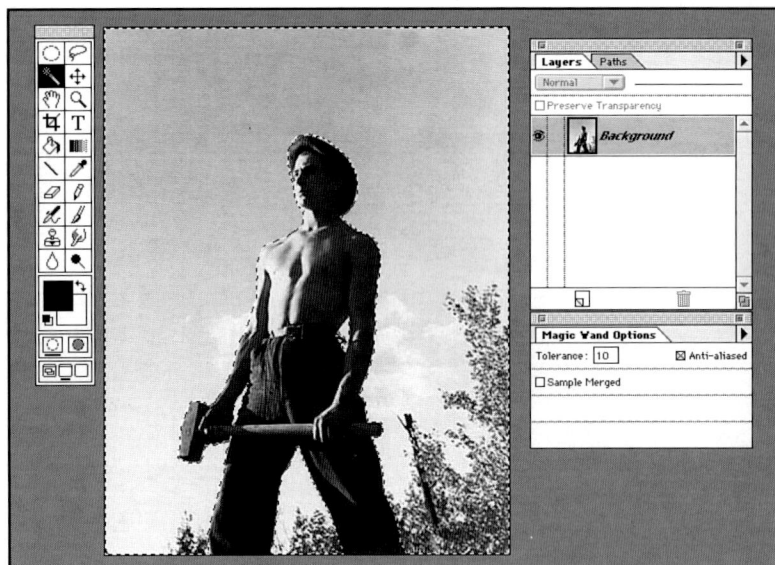

Figure 8.3 Image that has been silhouetted.

Adding Text

Text stimulates the left side of the brain, appealing to the cognitive and rational, whereas images move the intuitive and non-linear right side of the brain. Put together, text and images create a powerful form of expression. As the ancient Chinese oracle, the I CHING says, "Words cannot express thoughts completely, [therefore] the holy sages set up the images…"

Text can include headlines, subtitles, picture captions, and blocks of words. Text can be added to the image in a number of ways: over, under, around, beside, or wrapped. Words can easily be wrapped around silhouetted images. In multimedia, text can be bit-mapped, which means it exists as a graphic unit and is not changeable, or it can be databased, which makes it both searchable and changeable.

However it is used, text should be used sparingly and always with its relationship to the image in mind. Here are some general guidelines:

▶ Keep the text blocks under 60 characters long using 12 pt type and 18 pt leading (or an equivalent length using larger type and leading).

▶ Make the text readable, which might mean avoiding color combinations such as blue text on a black background or using complementary colors. Neon text that screams for attention can confuse and tire if overused. Blue backgrounds with yellow or white text are especially readable.

▶ Anchoring text blocks and headings flush-left on a vertical grid line makes it easy for readers to follow the content.

▶ Look at the way that comic books and comic strips use text, especially the way that dialog is fit into balloons. Words and images are effectively integrated using time-tested techniques.

▶ To avoid a stair-stepped appearance around the edge of each individual letter of text caused by the square edge of pixels, apply anti-aliasing. Anti-aliasing interpolates pixels between the edge and the background so the border of each letter is slightly softened. For hard-edged text that is already readable don't apply this technique. If text is part of an animation, anti-aliased text will result in a distracting halo of artifacts when moved across a non-uniform background. Avoid this by using aliased text when you employ animation.

▶ Use sans serif letters and wider spacing for easier reading.

▶ Make sure that the fonts you choose will be available on the viewer's computer.

Whatever you do with the text and words, be sure to test your results with objective viewers for readability and comprehension.

Image as a Doorway

In the digital world, a single static image can be deceiving. Instead of only being a "window" to the world, as an image is often called in traditional media, by the use of software and magnification capabilities and "hot buttons" it can become a doorway as well.

In the photographic CD-ROM "Explore the Grand Canyon," for example, which uses nearly 3,000 photographs taken mostly by photographer James Cowlin, "hot spots" are built into the canyon itself. As you click on any of these spots, new images or details of the existing image are brought up. (*Explore the Grand Canyon* was produced by Scott Jarol and The Coriolis Group. It is only available for Windows and can be purchased directly from the publisher at 800-410-0192).

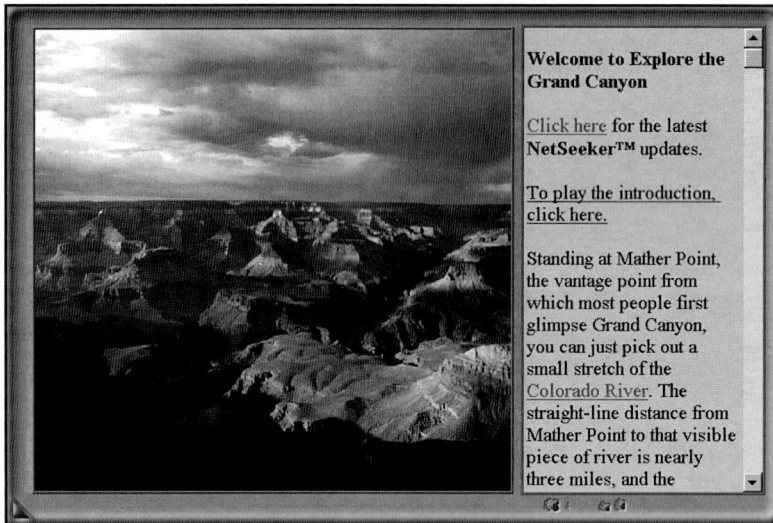

Figure 8.4   The opening screen from "Explore the Grand Canyon"—all photos copyright James Cowlin. The user can play the introduction as a self-running script with voice-over and music or the user can click on hot spots in the photographs and hyperlinked text to view the sequence.

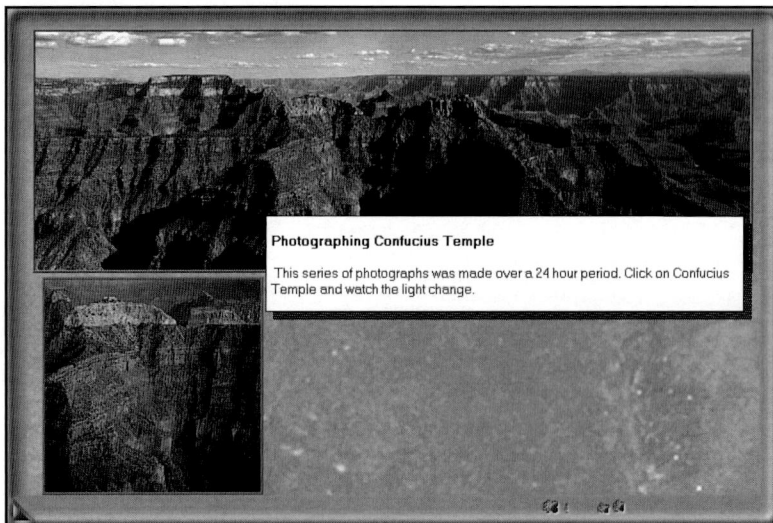

Figure 8.5   The first of a sequence of photos taken over a 24-hour period. At the top of the screen is a panoramic image. The prominent butte in the center is Confucius Temple. When the user moves the cursor over Confucius Temple it changes to a camera shape, which when clicked will change to the next panoramic in the sequence.

Figure 8.6   The next image in the sequence.

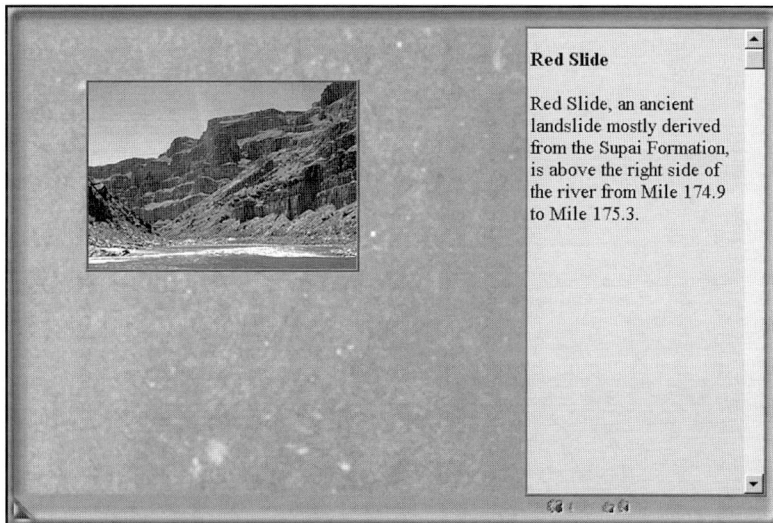

Figure 8.7   Red slide is a geological feature that is encountered along the Colorado River. When the user selects "Red Slide" from the hot spot on the topographical map, the first screen is displayed. Clicking on the prominent red structure in the photography brings up the second screen with close-up views of the slides.

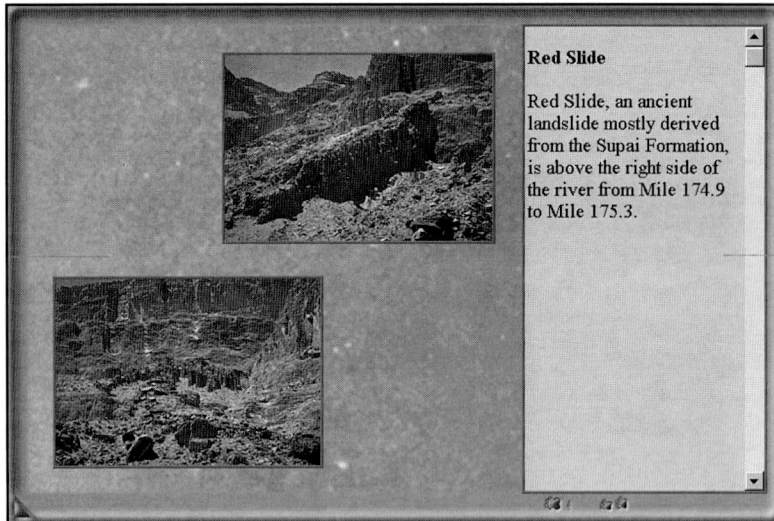

Figure 8.8 Another view of "Red Slide."

In "The Material World," another CD-ROM based on still images, magnification controls enable the viewer to zoom in to details of any photograph. ("The Material World" is based on the book by Peter Menzel. It was produced by the Graphix Zone. All rights reserved.)

Figure 8.9 An opening screen from "Material World."

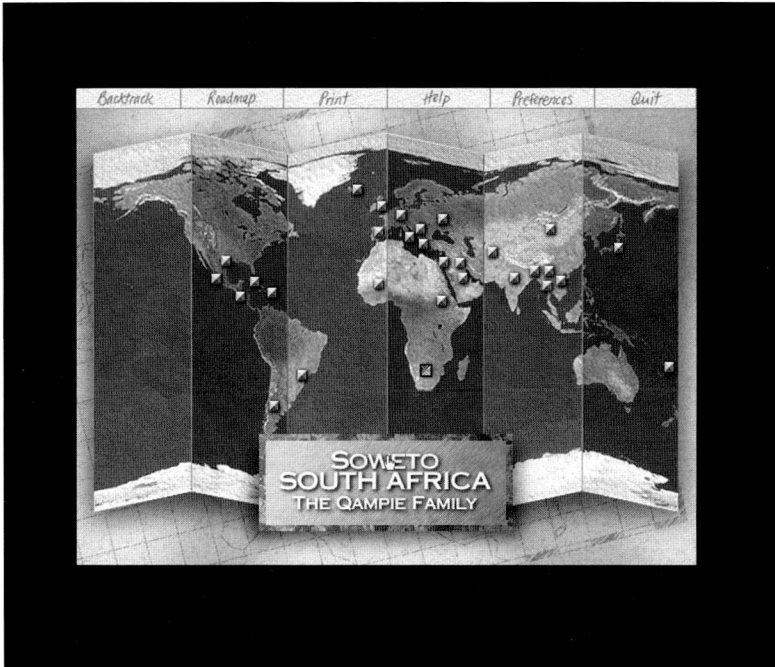

Figure 8.10   Viewers choose where in the world they'd like to go.

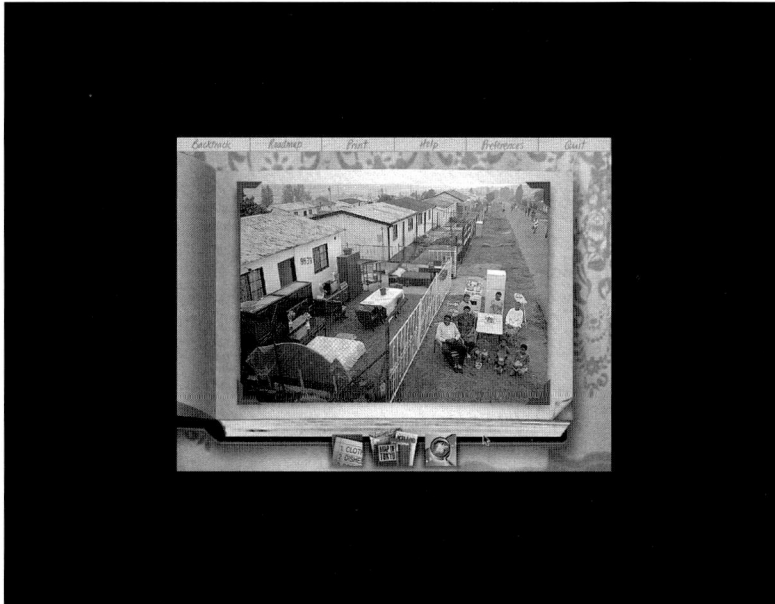

Figure 8.11   Soweto, South Africa. The Qampie Family, an overview.

Figure 8.12   A close-up of the family.

Image as Narrative

A digital image can also become a narrative. A still image can be brought to life through digital zooms into a particular point of detail, panning selectively around an image, or using other techniques borrowed from the film and video industry. Ken Burn's PBS series, "The Civil War"—80 percent of which consisted of still images—relied on this technique to achieve a dynamic effect as well as an all-time best ever PBS viewer rating.

TV and film producers use cinematographic methods or very expensive Avid or Avid-like editing machines to achieve these effects with still images. However, similar effects can be simulated using software such as Macromedia's Director or Adobe Premiere. You'll likely want to use these effects sparingly, because it doesn't take much to give a sense of movement to a still image. Also, you'll want to vary the effects. For example, pans starting from the upper right corner of an image can be followed by pans starting from the opposite side.

NOTE   With just a little experience, Macromedia Director can be used to produce zooms and pans. For a zoom effect, place a cast member on the stage where it now becomes a sprite. Select the corresponding cell in the score and copy the contents of the cell and paste it into a cell a few frames away. Now select the copied sprite on the stage, and using the Sprite Info box resize the sprite (the larger you make the sprite, the more dramatic the zoom). Now go back to the score and select the first and last cell the sprite is in as well as all the frames or cells in-between. Use the in-between linear command to complete the sequence and fill the middle cells. When you play the sequence, a zoom-like effect will result. (You can also control the zoom by writing a Lingo script that makes the sequence occur in the same frame, but this takes more work.) If you want to maintain resolution, use Photoshop to resize the image into stages (3–5 images) and then import each new image into Director and sequence them as subsequent sprites with fast dissolve transitions. To create a pan-like effect in Director, use Lingo commands to move the viewer's perspective in the direction you want—left, right, up, or down.

Image as Kinetic Sculpture

When a still image begins to move it startles and pleasantly surprises the viewer. Presenting the unexpected is always an attention grabber. There are many ways to make a still image move. Here are two examples:

▶ The design group Option X created a digital portfolio as a promotional piece for New York-based illustrator James Yang. By animating Yang's work, they gave the images a new dimension on the electronic screen.

Digital Yang was created using Yang's Illustrator files to create several variations, which were then imported into Director and animated. Analog Yang was created by digitizing Yang's drawings and using Photoshop to create a set of sequences that were then imported into Director and animated. (Some of the images are shown here. The entire piece can be viewed on the accompanying CD-ROM but is Macintosh-specific.)

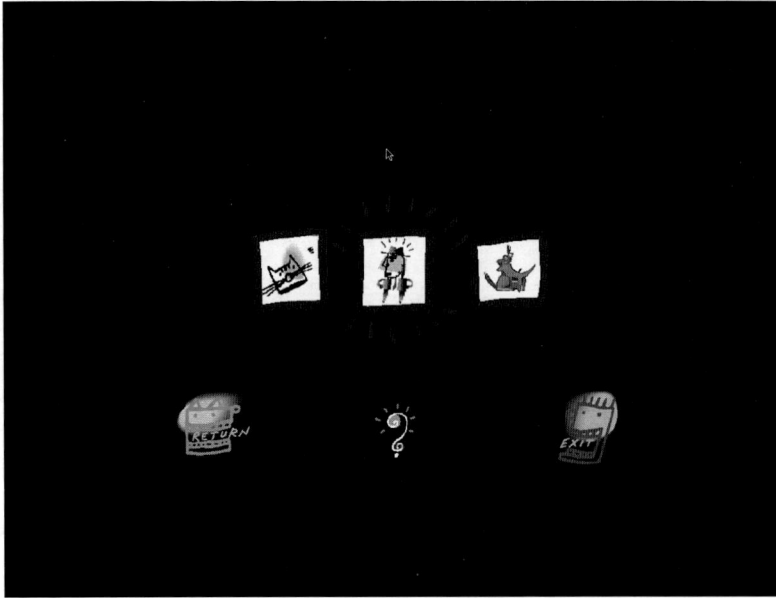

Figure 8.13   One of the opening screens from Option X's James Yang portfolio.

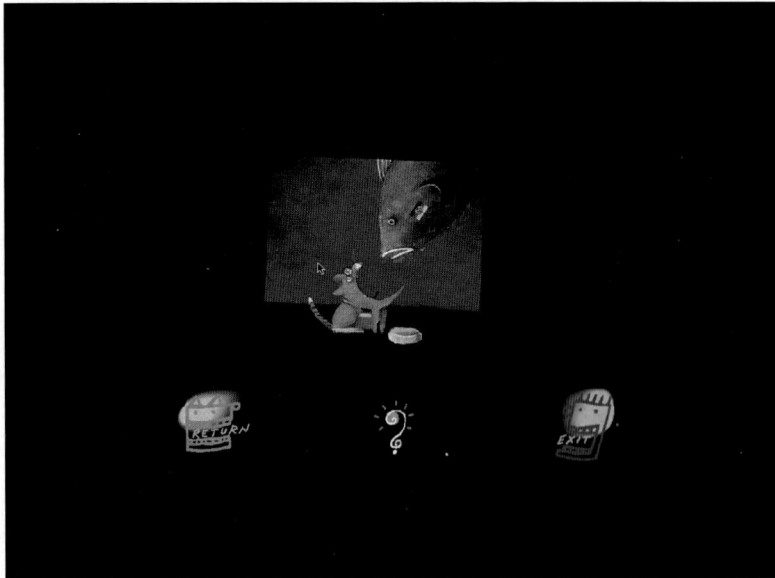

Figure 8.14   This started out as one of Yang's analog drawings. In the digital version—which you will find on the accompanying CD–ROM—the cat appears to be eating the fish.

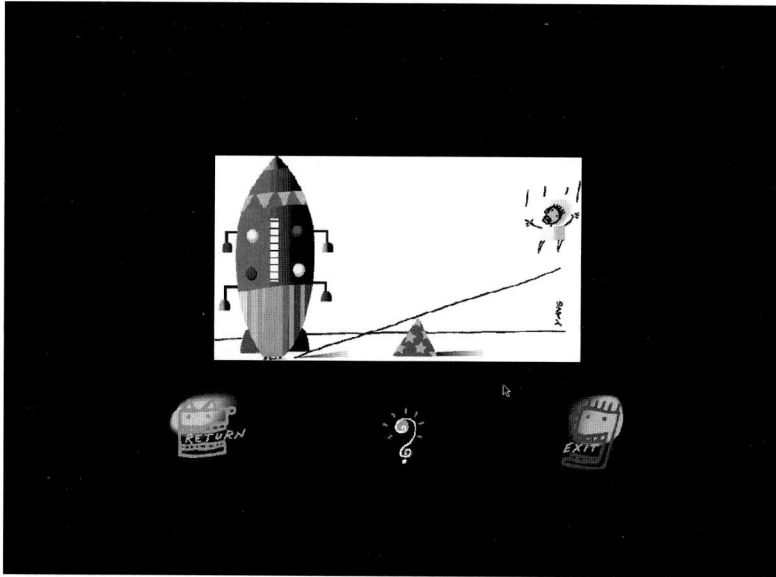

Figure 8.15   This began as an Adobe Illustrator file and for the digital version Option X made the rocket and the girl swing.

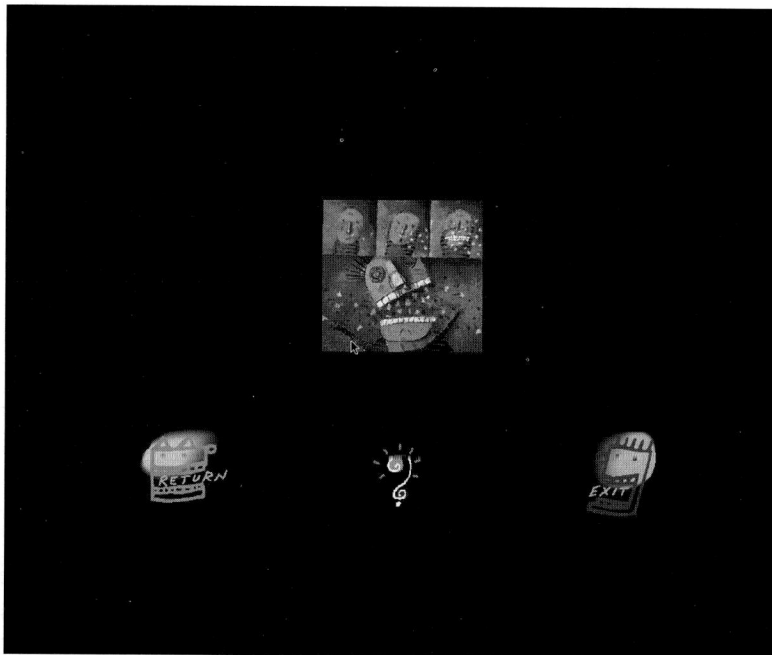

Figure 8.16   In the animated version, the man sneezes over and over again.

▶ Another easy way of making a still image appear to move without using a lot of memory is by the selective use of palette flashing. This is usually an accidental and unwanted effect, such as what occurs when two images with different palettes are on the screen at the same time. You can use this effect to your advantage, making a fire flicker, for example, or making water "flow."

(In Director, this is done by simply selecting a range of colors in the active palette. The screen will automatically cycle through these colors, giving the appearance of movement. You can also use Lingo's puppet Transitions command to make a still image seem to move.)

Image as Puzzle

Presenting a challenge to a viewer is another way of grabbing attention. In this example, produced as a Web page by Option X and the author, a still image created by the French multimedia artist Chris Marker was broken up into blocks. When the Web page is accessed, each block appears at random on the screen and the underlying image is not apparent. As viewers click on each block, trying to figure out what to do next, new pages appear teasing them to figure out the puzzle. When the viewer finally opens the browser screen wide enough, the image rearranges itself into the whole. The puzzle was created using Adobe's PageMill. (The site can be reached at the following url: www.his.com/~maaland/O.W.L.)

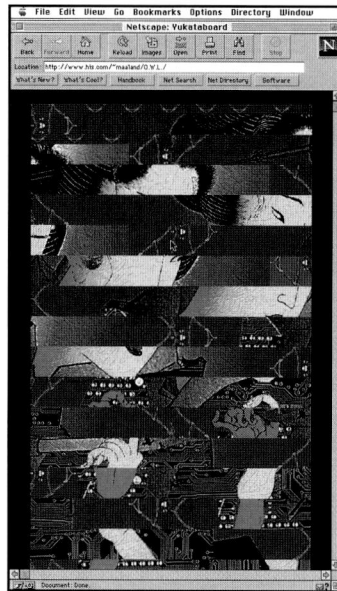

Figure 8.17 This is the opening Web page of the O.W.L. puzzle. The image is garbled and the viewer is encouraged to solve the puzzle. All images are copyright Chris Marker.

Figure 8.18 As viewers clip on the opening image they are linked with separate pages such as this one that provides clues to solving the puzzle.

Figure 8.19   Another clue.

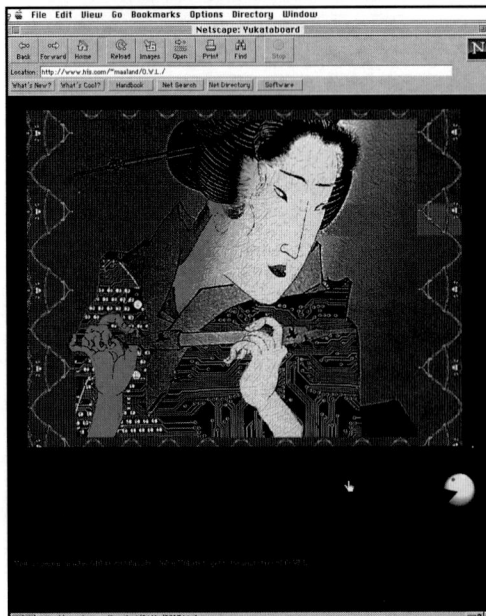

Figure 8.20   Once the viewer opens their browser to a larger screen size, the image snaps together and the puzzle is solved. A gateway to the next level is revealed and the viewer can move on.

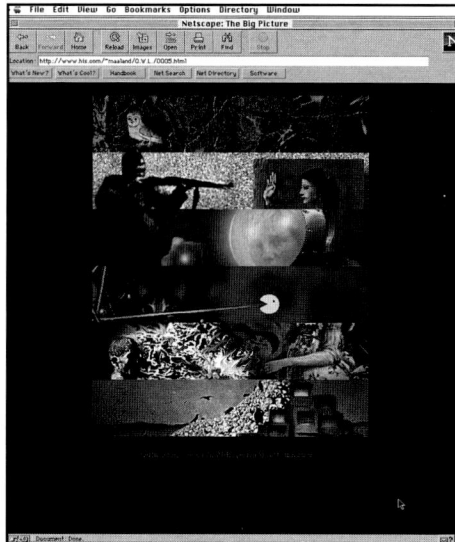

Figure 8.21   After the puzzle is solved the viewer encounters this visual menu that will lead them even deeper into the site. A "prize" waits for the viewer at the end.

Sequenced Images

Sequencing several images is a particularly good way of setting a mood, creating a narrative, and establishing a point of view. Sequences can exist solely by themselves or as segments within larger projects. When combined with sound (discussed at the end of this chapter) they become even more arresting.

Unlike full motion video, which uses a lot of computer processing memory, sequencing stills puts much less demand on your hardware, but can achieve an equivalent effect.

NOTE   A debt is owed here to three different professions—cinematography, photography, and comic strip illustration—which long before computer multimedia came into being, developed creative ways of sequencing stills. In the cinematographic world, sequencing stills is referred to as kinestasis, or moving stills (kine = moving and stasis = stills). One of the most famous films ever done this way was La Jetee (1962), which,

continues

continued

except for one moment when a woman's eyes flutter, was constructed entirely with still photographs. To the photography world, sequenced stills are known as multi-image slide shows, which were especially popular at trade shows, museums, and conferences in the 1970s. To the comic book strip industry, sequencing is just business as usual. In my opinion, no other profession has been as successful in overcoming the challenge of telling stories in just a few frames as these illustrators. Several books have been written describing the art of the comic illustrator (listed in the appendix), which I highly recommend reading.

Many off-the-shelf software programs allow for the sequencing of images, some with more control over others.

Case Study:
Curtis Wong/Corbis

Curtis Wong is the Executive Producer and General Manager for Corbis, in charge of creating the award-winning CD-ROM title "A Passion for Art" (excerpt included on the accompanying CD-ROM). Before coming to Corbis in the early 90s, Wong was on the ground floor of the multimedia industry creating video discs and CD-ROMs for Voyager. At Voyager he was introduced to the works of the photographer Pedro Meyer, which resulted in the innovative and groundbreaking CD-ROM "I Photograph to Remember"—a series of Meyer's still images sequenced and combined with voice-over and music. Wong often refers to that simple yet powerful project as evidence of the inherent value of still images in the new media.

Wong:

At Corbis, we don't find using still images restrictive at all. Look at what Ken Burns did with just still images on the "The Civil War." We find that when people shoot video and film they tend to be sloppy. Unless it's a major motion picture, a lot of film is simply a pan from here to there. A still image, especially studio photographs, or great historical photographs, are carefully crafted and capture a moment in time that you probably couldn't do if you were shooting thirty frames per second.

We plan to continue creating titles with a strong emphasis on narrative, using high-quality still images, all the while pushing the envelope in terms of interactive storytelling, trying to give the viewers the ability to choose their own path through the material. We are also looking into the innovative uses of panoramic navigable images complimented with ambient sound that you can explore and move around in. In "Critical Mass: America's Race to Build the Atomic Bomb" there is a section called beyond "Trinity" where images and music are juxtapositioned together either in a random fashion or orchestrated in a particular way by the viewer with the result being quite powerful. In both cases images and sound—and if the viewer wants, text—come together in very different ways and create unexpected results. As always, we are trying to give as much control to the viewer as possible, and still images help us do that.

Selection

Before placing the images into a program, it helps to photocopy them and place them side by side sequentially. Look for both literal and figurative relationships between images. See how the colors and tones relate. Try to sequence contrasting images together for effect. Imagine what the "third" effect might be if two images were briefly overlapped in a transition.

The Gutter

This is a term borrowed from the comic strip industry. The gutter is the unillustrated action between two frames. It is the space where the viewer uses his or her imagination to fill in the blank. Often the gutter is a moment in time between events. It can represent a minute, an hour, a day, or even years depending on the content of the frames on either side. The image of people riding in a carriage followed by the same people sitting in a drawing room requires the viewer to interpolate the time and actions getting from the carriage into the drawing room. Use the gutter carefully. Consider how much you are asking of viewers between frames. It is surprising how much people actually do fill in when a sure hand guides them. Test your results on others to ensure viewers do not become confused.

Timing

Timing is the speed in which sequential images appear on the screen. The actual amount of time that you hold an image on the screen will depend on the image itself and other factors such as sound or music. Images that you want to emphasize or images that emphasize a particular point should remain longer on the screen. Related images that imply motion should run more quickly. If used, music or voice-over will determine the speed and timing of images. Timing is largely a subjective decision that involves much experimentation to get it just right, although it will be clear when the timing is wrong.

Transitions

Transitions advance the sequence of images. They can do so with or without calling attention to the transition itself, depending on the overall effect you are trying to achieve. Transition effects—which are included in such programs as Director and Premiere—include fades, dissolves, and wipes. They can gradually or abruptly reveal another image or part of an image. A transition to a white or black screen can also be effective. Again, be careful with your choice of transition effects. There are many times when the best transition effect is one that just advances the images without distraction.

Backgrounds

A consistent background can be used to create a stylistic unity in your project. This is especially relevant if you are using images that are otherwise not related—that is, photographs combined with drawings, color images mixed with black-and-white images, and so forth. Backgrounds can be low-contrast photographs, simple patterns, or just a neutral color that doesn't distract the viewer from the actual images that lay on top of it.

Figure 8.22   Screen shots from the opening sequence of Corbis' "A Passion for Art."
The dramatic sequence was created by Ted Evans and EPG for Corbis.

NOTE Here is a really simple and inexpensive way to create a basic slide show of sequenced images from images that exist only as digital files on your computer. Set up a 35mm camera on a tripod in front of the computer monitor and shoot color slides or prints of the images directly off the screen. Process the film and transfer the slides onto a Kodak Photo CD. Now you have the images stored handily on a durable CD that can be played on your computer or on any TV set using special hardware available from Kodak and many other consumer electronic companies.

When shooting off of a CRT monitor: Shoot at less than 1/30th of a second to avoid showing the raster lines of the electron tube. Use a normal or slightly telephoto lens to minimize distortion of the screen. Mount the camera on a tripod and position the camera directly in front of the screen. Be sure to block out ambient light that might cause glare on the screen's surface. Use filters or change the color temperature of the color monitor to match the color film. Remember that most SLR camera viewfinders show only 92 percent of the area that is actually exposed on the film. Experiment and get to know your camera and film.

Adding Sound

Turn off your TV and try watching a program without the sound. Pretty boring, even with all that motion. Sound is one of the most underused digital design elements. Why? Perhaps because many people working in multimedia have moved from the graphic design world where sound just wasn't an option when the medium was paper. People coming from the world of video and film have long known that the surest way of improving poor-quality footage is by adding high-quality sound. (Studies have confirmed this only works one way: Good footage doesn't improve one's perception of poor-quality sound.)

Adding sound need not be hard. The same process that we have outlined for still images can be applied to sound: First you need to acquire the sound, then process it and place it in your presentation.

Sounds, like still images, can be found on CD-ROMs and on the Web. On the enclosed CD-ROM, we've included royalty-free sound samples from SFX's 2 CD-ROM set "Earshot," an excellent collection of sounds created specifically for the needs of multimedia producers. Increasingly, agencies that offer stock images offer stock sound (PNI through their Web site, Publisher's Depot, for example). In the appendix you will find other sources for finding sounds. As we have said earlier, sound is often copyrighted and you must obtain permission to use it. Getting permission to use music can take lots of time, so plan ahead and start the process early.

Creating your own sound can require no more than a microphone and a recording device. You can record directly into a computer by using special software recording software, or by using a storage device such as a conventional tape recorder or a Digital Audio Tape (DAT) recorder. You'll need a digital sound board on your computer (some come with them) and software such as Macromedia's Sound Edit 16, which is to sound what Photoshop is to images. You can also use as a source electronic keyboards and synthesizers that come with generic sound effects, such as hands clapping, animal noises, or weather sounds. If you have a large budget, you can consider employing the services of a recording studio.

The following are some ideas for creating your own sounds:

▶ Use a special keyboard dedicated to creating sound effects.

▶ Record "found" sounds, such as door slams, car engines, and train whistles.

▶ Simulate sounds such as footsteps and fire by the creative use of props. (Crinkling wax paper makes a good fire sound. Press your palm into a bowl filled with corn starch to simulate the sound of walking in snow. Use corn flakes for leaves rustling, and so on.) These effects are best created in a soundproofed room.

▶ Hire a musician or singer to create unique sounds or to play a song or create an original score. (Good guitarists, for example, can create an amazing array of sounds.) What you spend for their services could easily pale in comparison to the cost of licensing existing music or sounds.

▶ Use a professional for narration or voice-over. We all respond on a visceral level to the human voice, and how it projects will set a tone and mood for your entire project.

Once you have collected the sounds you want, think about saving them, thereby creating a library of sounds for future projects.

Processing the Sounds

Like a digital image, once sound is digitized it becomes elastic and malleable. You can create such effects as echo and reverb, or smoothen and change the tempo and pitch of a digitized sound. Besides the basic processing of sounds, you can also combine two or more sounds to create a "morphing" effect. You'll need special software to do this, such as Macromedia Sound Edit 16 or Opcode Systems' DigiTrax. To use the processed sound in your project, you'll need to convert it into a format that your presentation or authoring software can read. Director, for example, imports several types of formats including AIFF files for both the Mac and PC version. You'll also need to choose the quality of the sound, which is expressed as bits per unit, and the sampling rate, which is expressed in kilohertz (kHz).

NOTE   Use higher quality settings for music—16-bit audio, sampled at 44.100 kHz or less—and lower fidelities—8-bit at 11 kHz—for voices and other ambient sounds.

Virtual Reality

We are used to viewing still images that have tightly defined borders. But in looking at an image, haven't you ever wondered what lay beyond the edge of the picture, on the other side of that desk or window or person? Using new software programs such as Apple's QuickTime VR, the edge is no longer an edge. These programs literally stitch together a series of still images, creating, if you want, a 360-degree panorama that enables viewers to move as they want and even zoom into areas of the images.

This visual effect has immediate uses for creating games, educational and location-oriented multimedia titles, as well as for advertising and training.

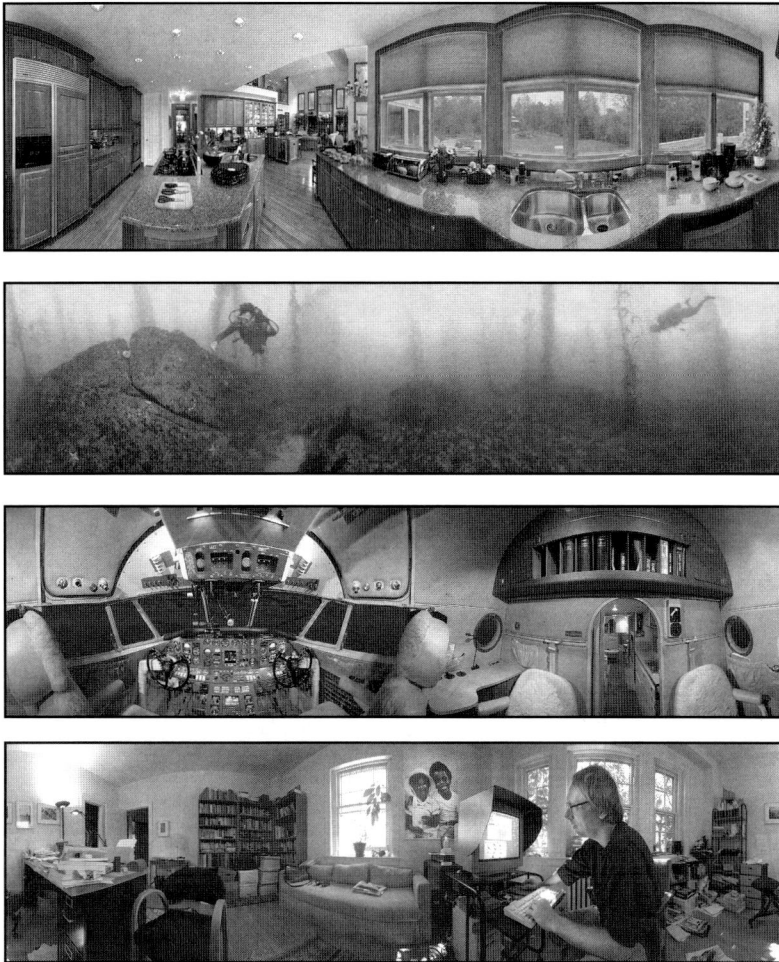

Figure 8.23 Photographer Scott Highton is one of the early pioneers of the VR technology. Initially hired by Apple to help develop ways of shooting and incorporating still images in QuickTime VR, Highton has since used his knowledge to help create several commercial titles including one for the Masco corporation. The first image was created for the Masco "Virtual Reality Showhome" CD-ROM, the second and third images were shot for Apple Computer, and the fourth image is a VR shot of the author at work. (All photos © Scott Highton.)

Case Study:

Ted Evans/EPG

Evans began his career as a cartoonist and painter, eventually ending up in design. Now he's part owner (along with Vince Peddle and Paul Gregritt) of EPG, an award-wining multimedia design company in Seattle, Washington. In the burgeoning world of multimedia design and production, Evans and EPG are renowned for their innovative use of still images to create entertaining and powerful stories. They created the opening sequence of the Corbis "Passion for Art" title, and are generally credited with creating the overall "feel" of the disc. They were also involved with Graphix Zone's' CD-ROM "Material World," based on photojournalist Peter Menzel's book, as well as several corporate projects, some of which are included on the accompanying CD-ROM. EPG has also created one of the first serialized interactive stories—titled "The Cypher"—a still-image ladened murder mystery spanning one thousand years, and which is currently running in "Launch," a CD-ROM-only magazine.

Evans:

Years ago I saw a multi-image slide show that used two slide projectors to project photographic slides on two screens with an accompanying sound track that played as the photographs were sequenced. It was a project for the American Cancer Society and it was the most moving piece I had ever seen. That's how I learned a still image coupled with audio could be so powerful.

Here at EPG we believe that the "old" multi-image model can be applied to CD-ROM projects. In fact, using still images for CD-ROM is a natural because of the limited processing speed of the computer. Full-screen video, after all, looks terrible. Using still images is our way of doing things.

We use the multi-image approach to create introductions or modules on a CD-ROM that whets the viewer's appetite for the rest of the title's content. For "A Passion For Art" for example, we wanted the viewer to understand that this was a story about a collection of great art that, except for a small group of people, had never been seen before. It was a great story, not only about the art itself, but about the people and drama behind the art.

We did a similar thing for "Material World." We used sequences of photographs to create a narrative about specific families from around the world. Through the images one sees different lifestyles and different ways of doing things. To accomplish this with film would have been very difficult and very expensive, and I don't know if it would have been as effective.

How do we pace our images? How do we combine the images with the sounds? It all comes from the gut. We start out by defining what we want to say by asking: What is our message? What exactly are we trying to say? For

"Material World" we looked through boxes and boxes of photographs and found the images that captured the right feeling. Then, using questionnaires and photographers' journals, we crafted stories about the families. We then scanned the photos and put them in Macromedia Director along with a rough music track. I just let the photos sequence and watched and listened as the music played. Sometimes I would let an image that was particularly powerful sit longer on the screen. Other times I would do a quick cut between four different images just to give a quick overview or feeling. There are no hard and fast rules to follow. I just followed my instincts. We usually laid the voice-over narrative last. At times, I felt like a conductor conducing an orchestra—I controlled the tempo, depending on what I wanted to say.

We consider ourselves first of all storytellers, and we apply this to our corporate projects as well. Communication is communication and the best way to get a message across is with a clever, fun, and memorable story. The best ads are often the simplest, but they get to something at the core of our being.

We always try to generate our own content since we like to have a fresh look, and you can't get that when you use the same sources as other people. We also try to keep a low overhead, which is possible when your core revolves around still images.

At EPG we've come up with lots of creative ways to sequence images. We go in and out of black a lot. We use audio to engage our viewer's mind even when there isn't an image on the screen. Then, when the image appears, it is quite startling. Of course the computer limits us, especially when compared with multi-image slide shows or television. It's hard to do a lot of cross fading because few computers incorporate more than one screen. We use the normal pixel dissolves and pattern dithers, but they aren't enough. We have come up with some techniques that are fun, using several frame animations to create very effective transitions. The result feels like a transition but in reality is a 5-frame animation. We've created montages that change very subtly, all done with pattern dithers that create a strange transparency between images as they fade one into another. It seems like the whole thing is throbbing.

We are trying to force the computer, trying to bend the technology to our knees, instead of bending our knees to it.

The irony is that when people look at what we have done, they think it is something really new, but the techniques we use have been around a long time. In reality it is low tech, not high tech

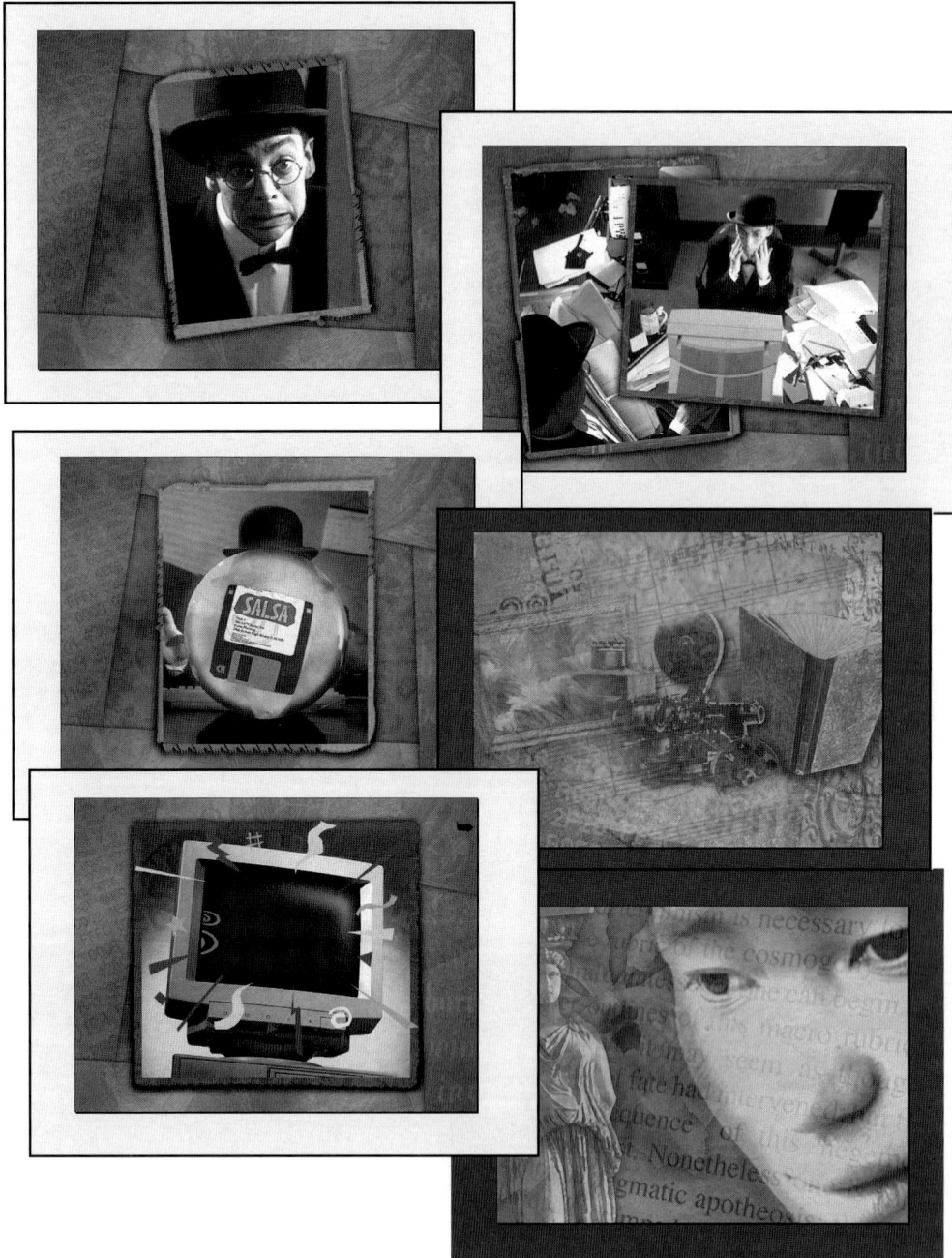

Figure 8.24   Screen shots from the works of EPG found on the accompanying CD-ROM.

IH027005.JPG

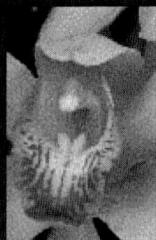
IH027030.JPG

IH027047.JPG

IH027135.JPG

IH027169.JPG

IH027216.JPG

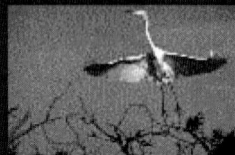
IH027358.JPG

IH027378.JPG

IH027489.JPG

IH027521.JPG

IH027539.JPG

IH027585.JPG

IH027605.JPG

IH027642.JPG

IH027649.JPG

IH027748.JPG

IH027843.JPG

IH027900.JPG

ih137641.JPG

copyright Corbis

Chapter 9

Still Images on the Web

The World Wide Web—the graphics-friendly part of the Internet—is both a multimedia-oriented medium and a low-cost distribution system that reaches instantaneously to all corners of the world, available 24 hours a day to anyone who is equipped with server service and software, a modem, and a computer system. Unlike a CD-ROM, which once pressed becomes immutable, images and information placed on the Web can be instantly shared and updated.

And yet, as either a publishing or distribution medium, the Web is not perfect. Limited by low modem speeds, even pages with simple graphics can take a long time to appear on a screen. Incompatible Web software (called browsers) make it difficult to predict exactly how your creation will appear on another system. The servers where you keep your creations can crash.

These limitations may change as bandwidth increases, software is standardized, and the Web matures. Full-motion video, 3D animation, and virtual reality may soon become common on the Web. But in the meantime—largely because of their relatively low bandwidth requirements—still images reign on the Web. (And frankly, I think still images will retain their primacy on the Web for a long time.)

If presented properly, a still image will add a universal visual appeal to your page. It can be read and appreciated by people all over the world. With some finesse and clever programming, you can even simulate many of the more advanced effects such as image sequencing and movement that we discussed

in Chapter 8, "Combining Images, Text, and Sound." On the other hand, if you add an image to your work without regard to the limitations of the medium, you'll suffer the wrath—or worse yet, indifference—of a viewer who has little time or patience to wait as your page slowly appears on the screen.

Here are the basic steps for preparing an image for use on the Web.

1. Acquire and process the image as you would for any multimedia project. (See Chapter 5, "Image Processing") Images should be examined for tonal qualities and contrast, then cleaned of scratches, dust, and noise from the scanning process.

2. Using Photoshop or DeBabelizer, resize the image and set the resolution to 72 dpi.

3. Choose a file format that compresses the image and is Web-compatible. At this time GIF and JPEG are your best options. Use JPEG for photographic images and continuous tone art, and GIF for line art, black-and-white photos, and illustrations that contain few colors. (More on this later.)

   For either format be sure to use the file extension .gif or .jpg when you save the image. Use lowercase letters, or your server won't be able to find the image.

4. If you choose GIF (pronounced either with a soft or hard g—you choose), you will have a maximum of 256 colors to work with—and less if you consider that the Macintosh and PC systems share only 216 of those colors in common. You will have to index the colors, selecting no more or less colors than are necessary, and selecting those colors that best represent your image. You'll want to avoid dithering if possible because dithering adds "noise" to an image and therefore increases file size. You also have no control over how a dithered image will look on another person's system.

5. Use the HyperText Markup Language (HTML)—the authoring language of the Web—to place the image on your page. HTML is a simple programming language to learn. If you use a Web authoring program such as Adobe PageMill or Vermeer/Microsoft's Frontpage,

the HTML translation is done automatically for you. Keep in mind that in the near future most presentation and authoring software will be "Web friendly" meaning they will do all the scripting for you.

Because most people will view your work using a 14.4 or slower modem, a good rule of thumb is not to use any image over 50 KB. (At least not until the Web's bandwidth increases and more people have faster access to it.) A 50 KB image will take only 10-20 seconds to download (depending on the speed of the computer and the server.) Even at this speed you might lose some of your viewers—especially the ones with a slower modem, so you will want to use some of the tricks mentioned in this chapter ("Keeping the Viewer Online") for keeping the viewer's attention as the image downloads.

The quality of a 50 KB image depends on several factors. How detailed is the image? How many colors? The spatial dimension and tonal quality that you want to run the image, the format in which you save the image (GIF or JPEG), and the amount of compression you apply will all affect the final look of the image on the screen.

You'll always have to make a choice between spatial and tonal quality: To run your images big, you'll have to choose fewer colors. Run it small, and you can increase the tonal resolution. What you do will depend on the type of image (line art or full color photograph) as well as your design considerations (big image with few words or several small images with lots of text). Keep in mind that when it comes to spatial and tonal quality, Web viewers are generally forgiving. They are not forgiving when it comes to download time.

Formats: GIF or JPEG

At this time, GIF, which stands for Graphic Interchange Format, is good only for images that are 8 bit (256 colors) or less. But with a transparent GIF you can mask and make invisible selected areas, and by using an interlaced GIF, you can make an entire image appear quickly but without all the detail, which is then gradually added. GIF only compresses an image by a factor of about 2, but with no loss of detail.

JPEG allows you to use 24–bit images and compress them as much as 20 times. (JPEG uses a lossy compression technique, which means quality is lost in the translation.) The more compression that you apply, the smaller the file size and the more image degradation. If you use Photoshop to create a JPEG file you'll have four choices of compression: low, medium, high, or maximum. DeBabelizer gives you many more choices. Whatever you do, be sure to experiment with different settings and view your results—each setting will compress an individual image in a different way and some settings will not be acceptable. At this time JPEG doesn't feature interlacing, which means that images will "venetian blind" from top to bottom, meaning the top of the image appears first then works its way down. (A new JPEG standard, called Progressive JPEG, displays an entire image—albeit blurry—at once and then progressively fills in all the details. This standard is not yet widely supported but will be in the future.)

Keep in mind that JPEG doesn't work with color indexed images—it works only with 24-bit color or 8-bit black-and-white images. Also, because of the way that the JPEG compression works—it blurs and softens sharp edges—it is not as good to use on images that contain a lot of detail or images that contain text.

Keeping the Viewer Online

Rarely is your audience *required* to look at your Web creation. You are competing with literally millions of other sites that are only a link away. It's not enough just to optimize an image so that it takes only 10 seconds to download. You need to use some tricks to keep viewers engaged. Using interlaced images is helpful. They give someone a quick idea of what the image will be like and a choice to stop the downloading early on. If you are using JPEG and the image builds from top to bottom, you might want to give some consideration to "top loading" an image. In other words, use an image with something visually intriguing at the top rather than one with, say, an empty expanse of sky.

Another good way of grabbing and engaging a viewer's interest is through the use of text. Text comes up nearly instantly on most systems and a viewer will naturally read it as they wait for an image to appear. If you create text that is interesting or builds anticipation for the image itself, a viewer is more likely to wait for the entire page to appear before zooming off to another site. (All that was said in the previous chapter about using text applies here—people generally don't want to read huge blocks of text on their monitors. Think in terms of short "teasers.")

Pushing the Limits

Here are some additional things that you can do to compensate for the graphically challenged nature of the Web:

▶ Create elements within your project that are downloadable. For example, as part of the Chris Marker Web site that we discussed earlier in the book, we created a sequence of 50 color images and captions, made a Director projector of the sequence, and placed it on an FTP site. Viewers using a 28.8 modem and a Mac could download the file in less than ten minutes and then watch our creation off-line at their leisure.

▶ Simulate movement by cycling pages or using multi-block GIFs.

▶ Link images to other images by using ISMAP invisible hot spots.

▶ Give the viewer the choice of seeing a higher resolution image by clicking on a smaller thumbnail version.

▶ To get the latest information and to keep up-to-date on the most innovative Web publishing techniques, check out the following Web sites. You'll get lots of great information on the best way of creating custom palettes, choosing formats, and using images on the Web. Lynda Weinman's Web site is particularly good. It contains a lot of material from her new book from New Riders, *Designing Web Graphics,* as well as a "Browser Safe Palette" download that contains the 216 colors that are used by both the Mac and PCs. Her address is: http://www.lynda.com/. Another good source is the Bandwidth Conservation Society's site, which gives lots of examples on ways to "slim" down graphics for use on the Web. Their address is: http://www.infohiway.com/faster.

Some day, as browsers and bandwidth improve, a Web publisher will be able to author Web pages in much the same way you've seen multimedia producers author other projects shown in this book. But even then, as you can see by the compelling projects following, Web publishing will be only as successful as the content itself.

Case Study:

Chris Vail, Time Inc. New Media

Chris Vail is a multimedia designer who uses news and documentary material to create forms of interactive electronic storytelling. Currently he is the Art Director for a new online service at Time Inc., New Media, designing Web sites for high bandwidth cable modem delivery.

Before coming to Time, Inc. Vail, along with Sue Johnson and Allison Cornyn, created Picture Projects, a Web site that currently features the Bosnia photographs of Gilles Peress. This site was created to showcase documentary work that emanates from strong personal conviction and to provide a forum for personal dialogue between photographer and viewer.

The elements that make up this current project, "Farewell to Bosnia," include the images of Gilles Peress accompanied by excerpts of letters he wrote during the months spent photographing the Bosnian tragedy of violence. The material is personal and intimate and employs a design philosophy that emphasizes the poetry and emotional content that lies therein.

The site includes the responses of individuals who visited the traveling exhibition of these images curated by the Corcoran Museum in Washington D.C. In various locations, response rooms were set up to allow people to write letters to the people of Bosnia or tape themselves in a type of video confessional. A selection of those responses are presented in the site.(The site's url: www.itp.tsoa.nyu.edu/~student/picture_projects/)

Vail:

We've attempted to use the Web to combine photography, sound, and text to create compelling narratives. To us, a narrative doesn't necessarily have a plot, but it does have a strong emotional thread. I think we definitely succeeded with the Bosnia site. When we look at the site's hit list we find that most of the people go all the way through the site 20–30 pages deep. This is unique for the Web because the average visit to a site is 3 pages deep. We are seeing people hooked on the story.

The amount of text we use is really minimal. But by parsing it out with the imagery and using the interplay between pictures and words, we've created a dynamic tension that seems to be very effective. Of course, the pictures do speak for themselves, but they speak in an ambiguous voice, which is the nature of a lot of photography. The words nail down meaning and give nuance to the imagery. Captions take a viewer in a lot of different directions, and the interplay between them and the images is a delicate balance between defining a moment and allowing it to play itself out.

For example, in the Bosnia stuff there is nothing in the narrative that relates directly to the images. There are two separate stories largely possible because Peress' photos are really more like an open-ended conversation than a defining statement.

When we designed the site, we wanted it to have powerful words that came up and grabbed the viewers' attention as they waited for the images to download. Even though we kept the image files small (30–50 KB) it still takes time for them to appear. We wanted to give the viewers the chance to use their imagination and make associations with other images in their minds—adding yet another cognitive layer to the piece.

To us it was very important to make it easy for a viewer to make their own connections throughout the piece. We wanted to create a space within the viewers' minds that allowed them to make associations. If we were effective, then 1 plus 1 actually equaled 3.

The Web medium is definitely limiting with its low bandwidth and all that—but as publishers and artists we have to keep in mind that our power doesn't come so much from the technology itself but from the way that we choose to put all the elements together.

PICTURE PROJECTS   react   info   gallery

you are damned if you don't,
condemned to repeat their hypocrisy.

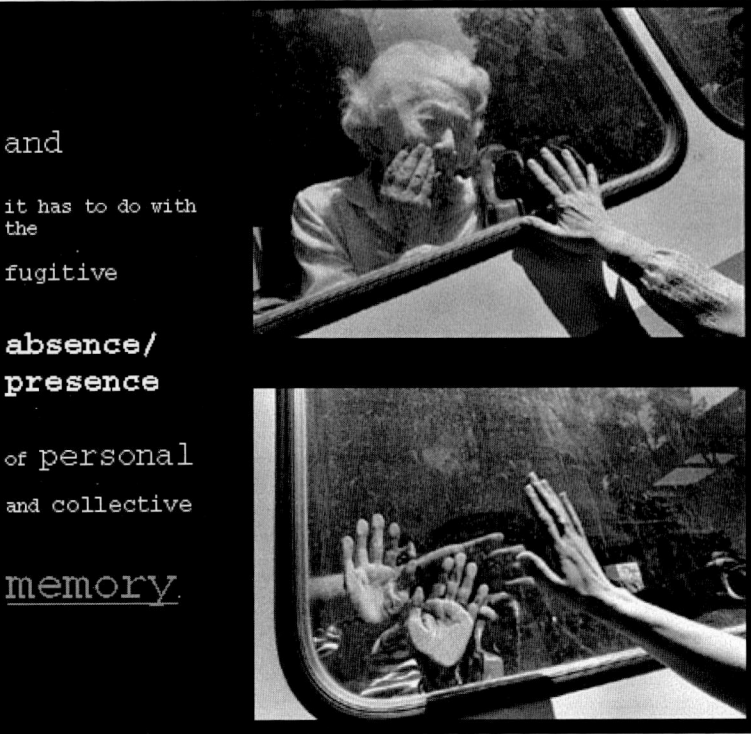

and

it has to do with
the

fugitive

**absence/
presence**

of personal

and collective

memory.

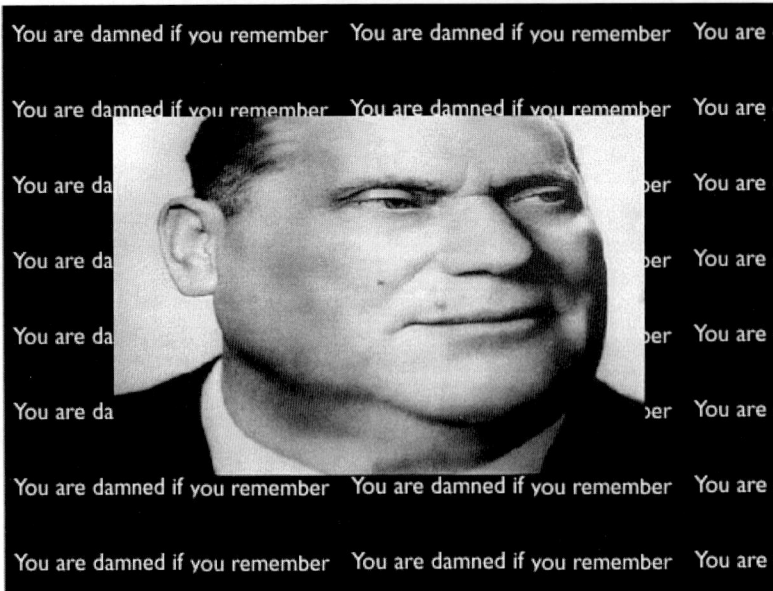

You are damned if you remember   You are damned if you remember   You are

You are damned if you remember   You are damned if you remember   You are

You are da   ber   You are

You are da   ber   You are

You are da   ber   You are

You are da   ber   You are

You are damned if you remember   You are damned if you remember   You are

You are damned if you remember   You are damned if you remember   You are

Figure 9.1 The Picture Projects Web site. All photos copyright Gilles Peress.

Case Study:
Tripp Mikich, Focal Point

Mikich is the former director of photography for the award-winning *Parenting* magazine. Along with Amy Howorth, formerly picture editor of *Wired* magazine, and Chuck Gathard, a photographer, Mikovitch founded Focal Point, a group dedicated to interactive journalism, using the new media to showcase innovative photography.

At first the group considered using CD-ROM as a platform, but then changed course after they made contact with Gary Matoso, a Paris-based photojournalist who proposed a photo documentary of a journey across postcommunist Russia. Focal Point decided that the Web would be the ideal medium for this project. Not only did it solve the problem of distribution, but they could update the site regularly as Matoso made his way across Russia. In September of 1995, with support from World Media, Sprint, Leica, and Kodak (who donated a digital camera), the site was created and the journey began. The transcyberian adventure took Matoso and Lisa Dickey, his writer traveling partner, 5,000 miles from Vladivostok to St. Petersburg and ended three months later. The "Russian Chronicles," found at Focal Point's Web site (www.f8.com), is a record of this journey. The site has received a 4 Star rating (the highest) by the Magellan/McKinley review. They wrote in their review: "Stunning photography, insightful commentary, and a smorgasbord of

continues

Case Study, continued

hypertext make Focal Point the leader in the burgeoning interactive photojournalism movement."

Mikich:

We wanted the site to be graphically simple. We created four main sections: "In Their Words," "Daily Chronicles," "Atlas," "Trip at a Glance," and "Road Stories." We chose small file sizes so the images would only take 10–20 seconds to download using a 14.4 modem. Every week we'd receive a transmission from Matoso and Dickey. Because the phone lines were so bad, it would take 4–10 hours to download 20–40 photos and 6–8 pages of text. Then we'd process and tweak the photos on this end (San Francisco), edit the text, and place the results in the appropriate section. Sometimes Matoso would send sound files and we'd link them to relevant words or text.

We wanted the site to be more than informative. We wanted to create a personal narrative, something that not only brought people in, but enveloped them and sustained a level of engagement. Viewers of the site were encouraged to email their comments to Matoso and Dickey, to give them real-time feedback. One Russian emigrant living in Canada emailed them and asked them to look up his family. They did and we posted pictures from the meeting and sound files from the kids. We like to think that we have taken photography from being a window into the world that evokes sympathy to being a door to the world that creates empathy and motivates people to action.

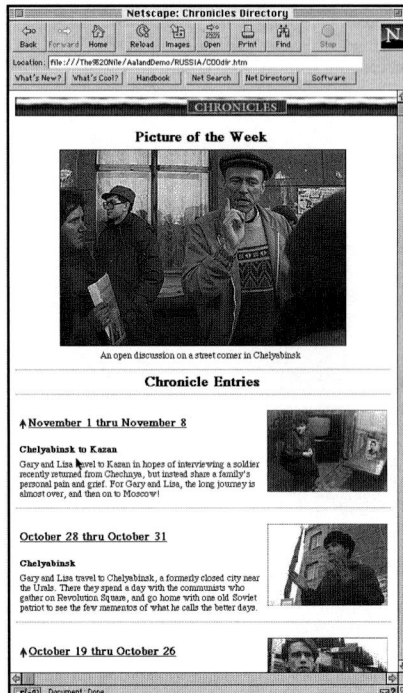

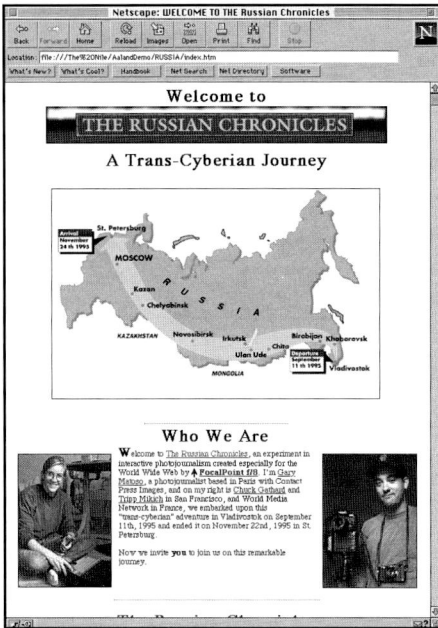

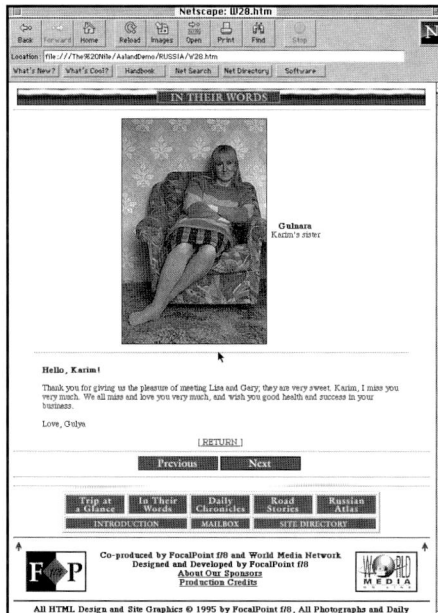

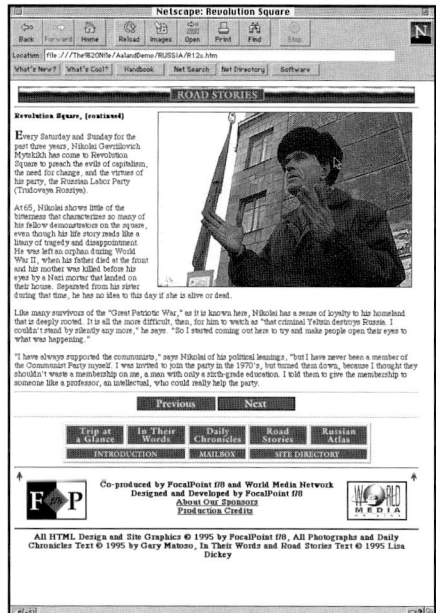

Figure 9.2   Screen shots from "Russian Chronicles." All photos copyright Gary Matoso.

Case Study:

Cynthia Carris, Picture Editor, Newsweek Interactive

Newsweek made the leap into new media in 1989 when they created a laser disc titled "Upheaval in China," an interactive piece on the student uprising at Tianamen Square. Since that project, Newsweek has created a half-dozen CD-ROM titles including "Open Roads: Driving the Data Highway," and its latest title, "A Parent's Guide to Children's Software." Carris, who has served as picture editor for several of the CD-ROM projects, is the picture editor for the online edition of Newsweek currently found on AOL.

Carris:

We have a section online where we run photo-essays. For this section I look for images that *Newsweek* would publish in their regular magazine if they had space. *Newsweek* has its own editorial look and feel and I honor that. As far as the actual image itself, I look for pictures that are really strong, that hold their own with just a short caption. If someone is going to wait for a picture to download, the picture better be good and have something to say. It can't just be a pretty picture.

Technically speaking, we lose a lot of detail when we put a picture online. If what makes a picture very special is its detail, we can't use it. Also, if the tonality is very subtle, it won't show up on the screen. I look for pictures where the action is close up, tighter images as opposed to wider ones. Images don't necessarily have to be centered. In fact for many images, it is the composition that makes them interesting.

I had a picture the other day that was great. It had won an award for print media, but I couldn't use it. It was an image of a girl running in Bosnia. She was running toward the camera, and it was a rainy, hazy day with a very white sky and you could actually see all the detail in the earth that she was running on. But you wouldn't have been able to read it online. A pity because it was a very beautiful image.

Do I think video will replace still images when the bandwidth gets greater? No. People said that when television first came out it would get rid of radio—and it didn't. I think still photography will always offer people something that they can't get any other way.

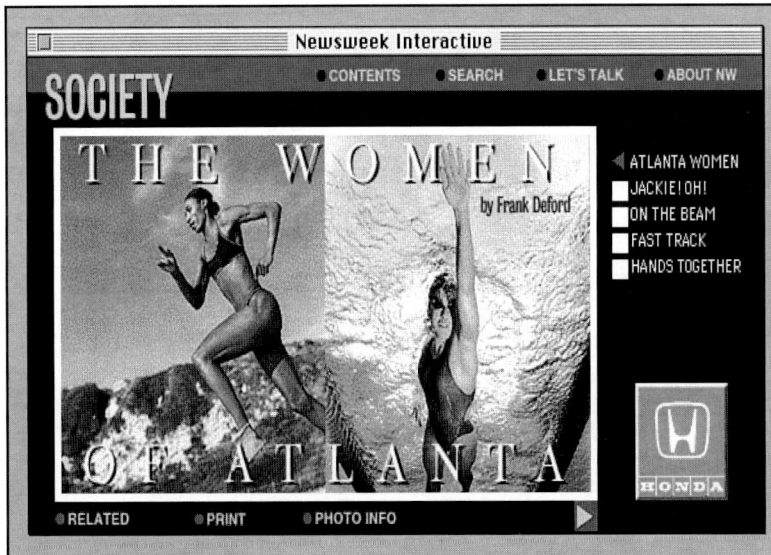

Figure 9.3 Newsweek Interactive's AOL site. Copyright Newsweek.

na007117.JPG DL001946.JPG a1028256.JPG ih000566.JPG

sc002278.JPG ih109313.JPG a1012983.JPG IH017808.JPG

th002198.JPG ih023053.JPG IH024436.JPG th002202.JPG

ih015249.JPG ih000552.JPG ih106585.JPG ih106651.JPG

ih106860.JPG ih107000.JPG ih109263.JPG rt006102.JPG

copyright Corbis

Appendix

Resources

General Bibliography

Adobe Photoshop Handbook, Photoshop 3 Edition, by Mark Siprut. Random House 1995. A best-selling handbook that's really good. Highly recommended.

Comics & Sequential Art, by Will Eisner. Poorhouse Press 1985. An intelligent and thoughtful guidebook written by one of the all-time masters of comic book art. Great tips on timing and combining text and images that are directly applicable to multimedia authoring.

Comics as Culture, by M. Thomas Inge. University Press of Mississippi 1990. Eleven essays on the influence of the comic strip and the importance of the comic book. More good stuff for the multimedia artist to know about.

Demystifying Multimedia: A Guide for Multimedia Developers from Apple Computer, Inc., by Randy Haykin. Apple Computer, Inc. 1993. A must-read for anyone wishing to become a multimedia producer.

Designing Multimedia, by Lisa Lopuck. Peachpit Press 1995. This author knows her color palettes! She also knows what else is important in multimedia production. Highly recommended.

Designer Photoshop (Second Edition), by Rob Day. Random House Electronic Publishing 1995. Updated to cover Photoshop 3.0's new features. Includes step-by-step examples of work by professional designers. Lots of step-by-step examples of techniques that are very useful.

Designing Web Graphics, by Lynda Weinman. New Riders 1996. An excellent book on the subject. Be sure and check out Weinman's Web site: www.lynda.com.

Digital Images: A Practical Guide, by Adele Droblas Greenberg and Seth Greenberg. Osborne McGraw-Hill 1995. An up-to-date guide on the general subject of digital imaging.

Digital Photography, by Mikkel Aaland with Dr. Rudolph Burger. Random House 1992. A basic introduction to the important concepts behind digital imaging written by the author in collaboration with an imaging scientist. Not product specific.

Everyone's Guide to Successful Publications, by Elizabeth W. Adler. Peachpit Press 1993. A fat volume full of to-the-point ideas. A successful step-by-step guide to the entire process of publishing, from planning to writing, to printing, to distribution.

I-Ching, The Richard Wilhelm Translation. Princeton University Press 1950. A book of wisdom.

Imaging Essentials, Professional Studio Techniques, by Luanne Seymour Cohen, Russell Brown, and Tanya Wendling. Adobe Press 1993. This is an excellent book for experienced designers and multimedia producers.

In Our Own Image, The Coming Revolution in Photography, by Fred Ritchin. Aperture Foundation, Inc. 1990. Written by the former *New York Times* magazine picture editor, this book is considered a classic work on the ethics and issues associated with electronic imaging.

Interactivity by Design, by Ray Kristof and Amy Satran. Adobe Press 1995. This book is tightly written and smartly designed. I found it full of helpful ideas.

Live Picture Revealed, by Josh Karson. Hayden Books 1996. Written by a photographer who collaborated with the designer of the innovative imaging program, Live Picture. The book is well-written and full of tips and strategies on how to use this powerful program.

Macromedia Animation Studio, by Gary Chapman. Random House 1995. If you want to use Macromedia Director to animate your stills, this book will show you how. It also includes a good technical section on using sound in multimedia productions.

Picture Research, by John Schultz & Barbara Schultz. Van Nostrand Reinhold 1991. The most complete book on this subject. Written by veteran stock agency couple who discuss extensively the legal and business aspects of picture research.

The Animation Book, by Kit Laybourne. Crown Trade Paperbacks 1979. I read this book ten years ago and I keep coming back to it for new sources of inspiration. It discusses every aspect of animation you can imagine, from the history, to the theory, to the actual practice of this venerable art.

The Presentation Design Book, by Margaret Y. Rabb. Ventana Press 1993. Written specifically for people needing to put together business-oriented presentations. Goes into great depth on ways to integrate images, charts, and graphics.

Type & Image: The Language of Graphic Design, by Philip B. Meggs. Van Nostrand Reinhold 1992. A lavishly illustrated book that discusses at great length the relationship between visual and verbal information. I like how it makes me think.

Understanding Comics, by Scott McCloud. Tundra Publishing Ltd. 1993. No one should be without this book. It is a must for anyone interested in producing multimedia.

Manufacturers and Developers of Digital Imaging Equipment

The following is a contact list of selected manufacturers and developers.

Monitors & Graphics Boards
Radius, Inc.
1710 Fortune Dr.
San Jose, CA 95131
408.541.6100
800.227.2795
www.radius.com

Scitex America Corp.
5120 West Goldleaf Circle, #10
Culver City, CA 90056
213.292.3600
www.scitex.com

Truevision, Inc.
7340 Shadeland Station
Indianapolis, IN 46256
800.858.TRUE
317.841.0332
www.truevision.com

Scanners and Scanning Software

The following is a contact list of selected scanners and scanning software.

Afga
508.658.5600 Extension 5808
www.agfa.com

Apple Computer, Inc.
1 Infinite Loop
Cupertino, CA 95014
408.996.1010
800.776.2333
www.apple.com

Hewlett–Packard
16399 W. Bernardo Drive
San Diego, CA 92127
619.487.4100

Light Source, Inc.
17 E. Sir Francis Drake Blvd.
Larkspur, CA 94939
415.925.4242
415.461.8011 (fax)
800.231.7226
www.ls.com

Microtek Lab, Inc.
3715 Doolittle Dr.
Redondo Beach, CA 90278
310.297.5000
310.297.5050 (fax)
800.654.4160
www.mteklab.com

Nikon Electronic Imaging
1300 Walt Whitman Rd.
Melville, NY 11747
516.547.4355
516.547.0305 (fax)
800.526.4566

Scitex America Corp.
5120 West Sololeaf Circle
Los Angeles, CA 90056
213.292.3600
www.scitex.com

Manufacturers and Sellers of Digital Cameras

The following is a contact list of selected manufacturers and sellers of digital cameras.

Apple
408.996.1010
www.apple.com

Canon
800.848.4123
www.canon.com

Casio
800.638.9228
ww.casio-usa.com

Crosfield
DuPont Printing & Publishing
800.538.7668

Dicomed
Dicomed, Inc.
800.888.7979

Dycam
800.883.9226
www.dycam.com

Fuji
Fuji Dealer Network
800.378.3854

Eastman Kodak
Eastman Kodak
800.235.6325
www.kodak.com

Leaf
Sinar Bron Imaging
800.456.0203

Minolta
201.825.4000
www.minolta.com

Nikon, Inc.
800.526.4566

Polaroid
800.662.8337, ext. 801
www.polaroid

Rollei
HP Marketing
201.808.9010

Scanview
ScanView, Inc.
415.378.6360

Service Bureaus

Many of today's computerized service bureaus are a direct outgrowth of photocopy ("Quick Copy") shops. The more advanced service bureaus provide access to desktop color scanners and color printers and can even support onsite color separations using a PostScript compatible digital typesetter. Service bureaus are commonly listed under "Computers" or "Computer Services" in the Yellow Pages.

Other Photo CD-Like Services

Kodak's Photo CD process for converting slides and negatives into a digital form is a preferred method among professionals. However, there are other low-cost ways of converting your analog material. In certain parts of the country, Konica, through commercial retail photo finishers, provides a low-cost analog/digital service. The resolution is much lower than Photo CD and the image files are returned on floppy discs that can be read by either the Mac or Windows. Picture Place, through AOL and CompuServe, will also convert your analog pictures into digital form and return the files to you via online or, if you prefer, on a disc.

Online Services

The following is a contact list of selected online services.

CompuServe Information Service
CompuServe, Inc.
5000 Arlington Center Blvd.
Columbus, OH 43220
800.848.8990

America Online, Inc.
8619 Westwood Center Dr.
Vienna, VA 22182
703.448.8700, 800.827.6364
or 703.448.8700 (fax)
www.aol.com

Prodigy Services Co.
445 Hamilton Ave.
White Plains, NY 10601
800.776.3449

Internet Access

The services previously listed provide Internet access. For other Internet access providers in your area look in the phone directory under "Internet Services."

Magazines and Newsletters

The following is a contact list of selected magazines and newsletters.

Communication Arts
410 Sherman Ave.
Palo Alto, CA 94306
415.326.6040
www.commarts.com

New Media
901 Mariner's Island Blvd., Suite 365
San Mateo, CA 94404
415.573.5170
www.hyperstand.com

Photo District News
1515 Broadway
New York, NY 10036
212.536.5222
www.pdn-pix.com

Digital Creativity & Pre
P.O. Box 4949
Stamford, CT 06907
203.358.9900
www.mediacentral.com

Future Image Report
1020 Parrott Drive
Burlingame, CA 94010
800.749.3572

Image Manipulation and Processing

Photoshop is by far the leading image processing software package for the Macintosh and Windows platforms. It's a full 24-bit color image processor that comes with a wide range of filters including image sharpening, softening, blur, a soft edge blur, mosaic, and diffusing. (Other special effects filters are available from third-party vendors.) Colors can be adjusted in several ways, including brightness controls, contrast, hue, and saturation. A histogram, to map the distribution of contrast throughout the image, is also included. Photoshop is an essential tool for multimedia producers wishing to use still images in their productions. Commonly sold for around $500.

Adobe Systems, Inc.
PO Box 6458
Salinas, California 93912
800.685.4169
www.adobe.com

Live Picture is one of the latest, and most powerful, entries into the image processing category. It utilizes a highly efficient file format called FITS. FITS, which stands for Functional Interpolating Transformation System, treats images as vector-based rather than pixel-based, in a resolution-independent form. Resolution-independent is a bit misleading. Even though a FITS algorithm easily doubles a picture's resolution with little or no degradation, you are still limited by the original scanned resolution. What this does mean, however, is when you view a part of an image on the screen, Live Picture dynamically refreshes the screen to give you full resolution at any zoom level. This program is ideal for large image files and for creating composites, but because of its limited filter support (among other things) it is considered a Photoshop complement, not replacement. Commonly sold for around $700.

Live Picture, Inc.
2425 Porter Street, Suite 13
Soquel, CA 95073
408.464.4200
www.livepicture.com
AOL:Keyword: Live Picture

Picture Publisher is an image processing program for Windows that is sold as a part of an extremely economical (under $200) graphic arts package called the ABC Graphic Suite. Considering its price, the program has many tools and options.

Micrografx, Inc.
1303 E. Arapaho
Richardson, TX 75081
214.234.1769
www.micrografx.com

xRes works with huge image files quickly even though it is not a vector-based program like Live Picture. xRes uses delayed and selective processing instead to speed up the creative process. Like Live Picture, xRes doesn't replace Photoshop but complements it in areas such as large file processing and painting and compositing. Commonly sold for around $500.

Macromedia
600 Townsend Street
San Francisco, CA 94103
415.252.2000
www.macromedia.com

Painting and Illustration Programs

I was once told that Photoshop is for the left brain and Fractal Painter is for the right. I like that description. This is a great program that takes some time to learn, but once you've got it, the creative juices can really flow. The latest version includes vector drawing, network painting, and special tools to create Mosaics. Commonly sold for around $400.

Fractal Design
Post Office Box 2380
Aptos, CA 95001
408.688.5300
www.fractal.com

If you plan on creating your own content, Illustrator (and other draw programs like it) are a must. Because it is a vector-based program, you can change or add to your creation at any time. Once an image is created using Illustrator, it is a straightforward process to create multiple variations and animate the image. Available for both Windows and Macintosh. Commonly sold for around $400.

Adobe Systems, Inc.
PO Box 6458
Salinas, California 93912
800.685.4169
www.adobe.com

Like Illustrator, FreeHand is a vector-based drawing program that boasts unlimited layering, editable blends, 100 levels of undo and redo, and lots more. Which is a better program, FreeHand or Illustrator? They are very similar in what they do and both programs are strongly supported by their respective publishers. It all depends on which program you are most comfortable using. For both Windows and Macintosh. Commonly sold for around $300.

Macromedia
600 Townsend Street
San Francisco, CA 94103
415.252.2000
www.macromedia.com

Sound Processing

There are lots of sound processing programs available, but SoundEdit16 is one of the most economical and useful. The multitrack document format allows you to edit unlimited audio tracks and output to any of 14 file formats and compression schemes. Comes with 18 special effects, four tone generators, and editing features. For both Macintosh and Windows. Commonly sold for around $300.

Macromedia
600 Townsend Street
San Francisco, CA 94103
415.252.2000
www.macromedia.com

Interactive Multimedia and Presentation Software Tools

The following is a contact list of selected manufacturers and developers of interactive multimedia and presentation software tools.

Presentation Software

Persuasion

Adobe Systems, Inc.
PO Box 6458
Salinas, California 93912
800.685.4169
www.adobe.com

Gold Disk Astound

Gold Disk, Inc.
2475 Augustine Drive
Santa Clara, CA 95052
408.982.0200
www.golddisk.com

Simple Image Sequencing Software

QuickShow

MetaTools
6303 Carpinteria Ave.
Carpinteria, CA 93013
805.566.6200
805.566.6385 (fax)
www.metatools.com

Museum
Rustle Laidman
PO Box 39A76
Los Angeles, CA 90039

Interactive Multimedia Authoring Software

Director, Authorware
Macromedia
600 Townsend Street
San Francisco, CA 94103
415.252.2000
www.macromedia.com

Claris HyperCard, Apple Media Kit
Apple Computer, Inc.
1 Infinite Loop
Cupertino, CA 95014
408.996.1010
www.apple.com

mTropolis, mFactory
1440 Chapin Ave., Suite 200
Burlingame, CA 94010
415.548.0600
www.mfactory.com

SuperCard
Allegiant Technologies, Inc.
9740 Scranton Road, Suite 300
San Diego, CA 92121
619.587.0500
www.allegiant.com

ToolBox
Asymetrix Corporation
110 110th Ave., Suite 700
Bellevue, WA 98004
800.448.6543
www.asymetrix.com

Other Related Software

Adobe Premiere, Adobe After Effects
Adobe Systems, Inc.
PO Box 6458
Salinas, California 93912
800.685.4169
www.adobe.com

Image Management Software

Prices will vary depending on the number of licensed users.

Cumulus Image Database is an excellent program that helps users manage thousands of images by creating a catalog that contains thumbnail images with index data and links to the actual image file. Indexing and Boolean search functions are easy to use. Different versions are available for single or multiple server use. (For Macintosh only.)

Canto Software
330 Townsend Street, Suite 212
San Francisco, CA 94107
415.905.0300
www.canto-software.com

ImageAXS is a software application for cataloging, retrieving, and displaying still and moving pictures. Automatic tiling and slide shows are built in. You also can create user-definable fields for textual data. All file information, keywords, and user-defined fields are searchable. (Available for Macintosh and Windows.)

DCI
1301 Marina Village Parkway
Alameda, CA 94501
510.814.7200

PICBase is a Windows database package for image management. Users are given control over the number of field headings, field titles, and field type. Search criteria are free form. Includes an image compression module.

Pegasus Imaging Corp.
4350 W. Cypress Street, Suite 908
Tampa, FL 33607
813.875.7575

Fetch is a Macintosh-based program that enables a graphic professional to catalog and retrieve archive images. Capable of holding 1,000 thumbnail views and 100 full-page views. Accepts multiple file formats. List price $295.

Adobe Systems, Inc.
PO Box 6458
Salinas, California 93912
800.685.4169
www.adobe.com

Color Calibration Software

Eastman Kodak's ColorSense Color Management Tool is a hardware/software package for under $500 that automatically maintains color consistency from input to display to output. The software coordinates peripherals so that they speak the same language and simulates how the displayed color will look when printed. The hardware calibrates your monitor for consistent screen display. The software works with TIFF, RGB, PICT2, and Photo CD formats and performs batch color processing. It also facilitates exchange of color data with service bureaus.

Eastman Kodak
343 State Street
Rochester, NY 14650
800.235.6325
www.kodak.com

Agfa's FotoFlow consists of four software modules—FotoTune, FotoReference, FotoScreen, and FotoLook—which work together to orchestrate consistent color from input to display to output. FotoScreen automatically color corrects and color separates images. Using a reference target, FotoTune creates a "ColorTag" and a "ColorLink" which help you color calibrate the entire process from input to output. It also allows you to translate colors from one color space to another, for example from RBG to CMYK. FotoReference is a software package for color calibrating scanners, and FotoLook is a Photoshop plug-in software module that provides output simulation of hardcopy printing devices on your monitor.

Afga
508.658.5600 Extension 5808
www.agfa.com

Compression

The following is a contact list of selected compression utilities.

Compact Pro
Cyclos
P.O. Box 31417
San Francisco, CA 94131–0417

Disk Doubler
Symantec Corp.
10201 Torre Ave.
Cupertino, CA 95014
800.441.7234 or 800.626.8847 (in CA)

PicturePress
Storm Technology
1861 Landings Dr.
Mountain View, CA 94043
415.691.6600 or 800.275.5734
415.691.9825

Stuffit Deluxe
Aladdin Systems, Inc.
165 Westridge Dr.
Watsonville, CA 95076
408.761.6200
408.761.6206 (fax)

ZipIt (PC)
ZIPIT.SIT
Shareware available on the Web or on CompuServe

Filters and Plug-Ins

The following is a contact list of selected maufacturers of filters and plug-ins.

Gallery Effects
Adobe Systems, Inc.
PO Box 6458
Salinas, California 93912
800.685.4169
www.adobe.com

Andromeda Photography Series
Andromeda Software, Inc.
849 Old Farm Road
Thousand Oaks, CA 91360
800.547.0055

HSC Convolver, Kai's Power Tools
MetaTools
6303 Carpinteria Ave.
Carpinteria, CA 93013
805.566.6200
805.566.6385 (fax)
www.metatools.com

Kodak Photo CD Acquire
Eastman Kodak Co. CD Imaging
343 State Street
Rochester, NY 14650
716.724.4000 or 800.242.2424

Photomatic
DayStar Digital
5556 Atlanta Highway
Flowery Beach, GA 30542
404.967.2077 Extension 243
404.967.3018

Watermark
John Dykstra Photography
4788 Anderson Lane
St. Paul, MN 55126
jdykstra@aol.com

Photo CD (and related Photo CD products)
Eastman Kodak Co.
343 State Sreet
Rochester, NY 14650
800.235.6325

Utilities

JAG II removes jagged edges from pictures and text. Batch processing is possible. Commonly available for around $90.

Ray Dream, Inc.
1804 N. Shoreline Blvd.
Mountain View, CA 94043
415.960.0768
415.960.1198 (fax)

DeBabelizer is an essential program for anyone using still images in multimedia. (For Macintosh only—Windows version expected soon.) The full version is commonly available for around $300.

Equilibrium
475 Gate Five Road, Suite 225
Sausalito, CA 94965
415.332.4343
www.equilibrium.com

Resources for Finding and Caring for Content

Besides using the resources listed here, you can go onto the World Wide Web and search using key words such as stock sound or stock content. This will lead you to further resources that will be immediately available.

Many public domain images also can be found on the Web. To find sites that offer these images use a search engine and enter the key words: public domain photography (or art). Be sure to check out the Library of Congress for public domain images (http://www.loc.gov).

Commercial Image Content Providers

The following is a contact list of selected image content providers.

Bettmann (Owned by Corbis)
902 Broadway, 5th Floor
New York, NY 10010
212.777.6200
www.corbis.com

Comstock, Inc.
30 Irving Place
New York, NY 10003
212.353.8600 or 800.225.2727

Corbis
15395 SE 30th Place, Suite 300
Bellevue, Washington 98007
206.641.4505
www.corbis.com

Corel Corp.
1600 Carling Ave.
Ottawa, Ontario
Canada K1Z 8R7
613.728.8200 or 800.772.6735
www.corelnet.com

Culver Pictures, Inc.
150 West 22nd Street, #300
New York, NY 10011
212.645.1672

Dover Publications (Reference for books with copyright-free art)
31 East Second Street
Mineola, NY 11501
516.294.7000

FPG International Corp.
32 Union Square East
New York, NY 10003-3295
212.777.4210
sales@fpgintl.com

The Image Bank, Inc.
2777 Stemmons Freeway, Suite 600
Dallas, TX 75207
214.863.4900

Image Club Graphics, Inc.
729 Twenty Fourth Ave. Southeast
Calgary, Alberta
Canada, T2G 5K8
403.262.8008 or 800.661.9410
www.imageclub.com

Letraset USA
40 Eisenhower Drive
Paramus, NJ 07652
201.845.6100 or 800.343.8973
www.letraset.com

MP©A
14 Washington Road, Suite 502
Princeton Junction, NJ 08550
609.799.8300

PhotoDisc, Inc.
2013 4th Ave., Suite 402
Seattle, WA 98121
206.441.9355 or 800.528.3472
www.photodisc.com

Picture Network International (Publisher's Depot)
2000 14th Street North, Suite 600
Arlington, VA 22201
800.764.7427
www.publishersdepot.com

PressLink
11800 Sunrise Valley Dr., Suite 1130
Reston, VA 22091
703.758.1740
www.presslink.com

The Stock Market
360 Park Ave. South, 16th Floor
New York, NY 10010
212.684.7878

Tony Stone Images
500 N. Michigan Ave., Suite 1700
Chicago, IL 60611
312.644.7880 or 800.234.7880
info@tonystone.com
www.tonystone.com

Sound Clip Providers

The following is a contact list of selected sound clip providers.

Sound Ideas
105 West Beaver Creek, Unit 4
Richmond Hill, Ontario
Canada L4B 1C6
800.387.3030 (US)
800.665.3000 (Canada)
www.sound-ideas.com

SFX
350 Townsend Street, Suite 403
San Francisco, CA 94107
415.243.0394
800.933.6223

References to Picture Sources

Anderson, Hilda. *The Travel Photo Source Book*. Washington, DC: Society of American Travel Writers, 1990. Annual publication listing travel photographs for sale and public relations sources.

Bradshaw, David N. and Catherine Hahn. *World Photography Sources*. New York: Directories, Jean C. Bradshaw, 1982. Listing of worldwide picture sources.

Brinzer, Dieter. *Photo Agencies and Libraries*. Baden-Baden, FRG: Presse Information Agentur GmbH, 1986. International resource for data about picture agents, professional organizations, photographers, and picture sources.

Eakins, Rosemary. *Picture Sources UK*. London: Macdonald and Co., 1985. Lists picture source collections in the UK.

Evans, Hilary and Mary Evans. *Picture Researcher's Handbook*. Berkshire, England: Van Nostrand Reinhold (UK), 1990. Listings of picture collections, with an emphasis on European sources.

McDarrah, Fred W. *Stock Photo Deskbook*. New York: Photographic Arts Center, 1989. Guide to foreign sources and individual photographers.

Robl, Ernest H., editor. *Picture Sources 4*. New York: Special Libraries Association, 1983. Lists many non-commercial and most commercial sources in the U.S.

Museums and Public Archives

National Aeronautics and Space Administration. *Photography Index*. Washington, DC: NASA, Public Affairs Division, 1983. Index to photography and artwork of the first manned orbits, trips to the moon, and other historic events of the U.S. space program.

American Association of Museums. *The Official Museum Directory.* Washington, DC: American Association of Museums, and Wilmette, IL: National Register Publishing Co., 1990. Listing of more than 6,000 museums in the U.S., revised annually.

Art in America. *Guide to Galleries, Museums, Artists.* New York: Brant Art Publications, 1990. Comprehensive guide to contemporary art and artists, published annually by the art magazine *Art in America.*

Museums of the World. Munich: K.G. Saur Verlag, 1981. Listing of major museums of the world.

National Historical Publications and Records Commission. *Directory of Archives and Manuscript Repositories in the United States.* Washington, DC: National Archives and Records Service and General Services Administration, 1978. Guide to more than 3,000 small and larger collections around the U.S.

Smith, Betty Pease. *Directory of Historical Agencies in North America.* Nashville, TN: American Association for State and Local History, 1986. Listing of over 9,000 historical agencies in the U.S. and Canada, mentioning photographic collections in many cases.

Vogt-O'Connor, Diane. *Guide to Photographic Collections at the Smithsonian Institution, Volume 1.* Washington, DC: Smithsonian Institution, 1989. Contains descriptions of more than three million pictures found in the Smithsonian.

Goodrum, Charles A. *Treasures of the Library of Congress.* New York: Harry N. Abrams, 1980. General information about the Library of Congress' collections.

Guide to the Archives and Manuscripts in the U.S. National Archives. Washington, DC: National Archives and Records Service, 1974. Complete listing of collections found in the National Archives.

Melville, Annette. *Special Collections in the Library of Congress.* Washington, DC: Library of Congress, 1980. Listing and descriptions of 269 special collections in the Library of Congress.

Visual Arts and the Law

Crawford, Tad. *Legal Guide for the Visual Artist: The Professional's Handbook.* New York: Madison Square Press, 1987. Legal guide for photographers and other visual artists.

Feldman, Franklin, Stephen E. Weil, and Susan Duke Biederman. *Art Law, Rights and Liabilities of Creators and Collectors.* Boston: Little, Brown, 1986. Describes the major issues in art law.

Care of Images

Time-Life Books. *Caring for Photographs: Display, Storage, Restoration.* Alexandria, VA: Time-Life Books, 1982. How to restore photographs and process them for archival storage.

Membership Directories (to track individual image providers)

American Society of Media Photographers (ASMP), 14 Washington Road, Suite 502, Princeton Junction, NJ 08550. 609.799.8300

British Association of Picture Libraries and Agencies (BAPLA), 13 Woodberry Crescent, Muswell Hill, London N10 1PJ, England.

Bund Freischaffender, Foto-Designer e.V (BFF), BFF-Geschaeftsstelle, Heilwigstrasse 67, D-2000 Hamburg 20, Germany.

National Press Photographers Association (NPPA), 3200 Croasdaile Drive, Suite 306, Durham, NC 27705. 800.289.6772

Picture Agency Council of America (PACA), PO Box 308, Northfield, MN 55057. 800.457.7222 Internet: PACA @ Earthlink.com

Finding a Picture Editor

The picture editor/researcher is a professional who can help you decide many things: when to hire an illustrator or photographer or when to use existing images. They know how to contact the right sources and can save you both time and agency service fees. Often, they know what rights and permissions need to be obtained. They are used to handling valuable properties. They can really make the difference between a chaotic project and one that runs smoothly. To obtain a reference for a professional in your area contact:

American Society of Picture Professionals. 2025 Pennsylvania Avenue NW Suite 226 Washington, DC 20006. 202.223.8442, 202.223.0034 (Fax)

Getting Legal Help

For a listing of further resources and references to professionals who can help you to obtain copyright and clearances do a Web search using Altavista or Yahoo (or other such search engines) and use the key words: legal, copyright, intellectual properties clearances. You can also checkout the following site for more information on multimedia and legal issues: www. dorsai.org/ p-law/ p-law 1.html.

Afterword

At this point, your project is finished and resides on a computer as a digital file. You may plan to have it pressed on a CD-ROM or placed on a Web site. If so, you—or someone you've hired—still has a lot of work left formatting and testing before the actual pressing of the CD. Then, if it is a commercial product, you have to market and distribute it. If you are placing your work on the Web, the work ahead of you ranges from simple if you are putting it onto someone else's server, to complex if you are setting up your own server from scratch. Alternatively, if you have created a presentation meant for a single monitor, once you've tested your project a couple of times and gotten feedback from a few people, you are basically ready to go.

In any case, without getting into the myriad of different tasks each approach demands, here are a few final words on the process of showing and distributing your work.

If you are presenting your work to a group:

- ▶ No matter how many times you have given your presentation, always test your computer, the projector, and sound system at least a day before you give your presentation.

- ▶ Always carry a backup of your file.

- ▶ If you are using someone else's computer, it's likely that the video card, fonts, palettes, and extensions you need won't be available.

- ▶ If you are traveling overseas, plan for different voltages, operating systems, and hardware connectors.

▶ Consider the conditions of the room in which you will be showing your work. Will the projection system be strong enough if there is a lot of daylight?

The final words on giving presentations with new media come from Steve Jobs, co-founder of Apple Computer and founder of Next, who once said that the chances of a software or hardware failure rise in direct proportion to the number of people in the audience. The author has proven this true on several occasions!

If you have created a CD-ROM for commercial distribution, have you:

▶ Tested your project on write-once discs across a reasonable selection of hardware/software combinations that users are likely to own?

▶ Made sure that the "Golden Master" disc, the final disc that is sent to a CD-ROM duplication service, has been thoroughly tested and de-bugged? It's a good idea to create two Golden Master discs, one that you send for duplication, the other that you keep as a backup. (As long as you have the second Golden Master, you might as well continue testing it until you know a final master disc has been cut and the duplication process has begun. You can never test too much!)

▶ Worked out the distribution? Retail distribution is extremely expensive and difficult to obtain.

▶ Installed a hot line for the torrent of questions that will come when your viewers can't install the CD-ROM or make it work? You can also hire an offsite company to do this job for you or just use email to answer questions.

If you are ready to put your work up as a Web page or Web site, have you:

▶ Obtained a Universal Resource Locator (URL) address that isn't a mile long?

▶ Found a server that is reliable?

▶ Prepared yourself for no one visiting your site?

▶ Prepared yourself for the possibility of a system crash to occur when you are demonstrating your site to an audience or someone you are trying to impress?

▶ Thought of other sites that you want to be linked with? It takes time and effort to establish Web "relationships" and to convince others to make the effort to include a link to your site.

One thing remains unequivocally true in the high-tech world of computers and multimedia: Always be prepared for the unexpected. And when things go right, count your blessings!

Index

A picture's worth a thousand words.

We have seventeen million pictures.

You do the math.

CORBIS

Upgrade To The Director Multimedia Studio 2 For Only $499.

Feel the awesome multimedia power of Director,® Extreme 3D,™ SoundEdit™ 16 plus DECK II™ (or Sonic Foundry's Sound Forge™ for Windows), and Macromedia xRes™ for only $499.** For first time buyers, it's all just $999.***

Upgrade To Director 5 For $399!

Get the most powerful multimedia authoring tool in the world for just $399.**

Get The Most Powerful Tools In Graphics And Design, All For Just $599.***

Design in 2D and 3D, create and modify fonts, and edit hi-res images with the new, integrated FreeHand Graphics Studio.™ Includes FreeHand,™ Extreme 3D, Fontographer,® and Macromedia xRes. Windows introductory price $449.***

Ready-to-Use Content for Both Mac and PC
(Certain restrictions apply)

175 historical and contemporary images provided by Corbis, the world's premier image content provider. (For personal use and exploration only.)

50 Royalty-free photographs by the author.

50 MB of Royalty-free multimedia sound clips from the EARSHOT CD-ROM collection by DXM.

Sample Multimedia Titles

Passion for Art (Corbis)—Mac and Windows

Russian Chronicles (Focal Point)—Mac and Windows—Open "Index.htm" from a Netscape browser

EPG Demos—Mac only

Software Demos
(some fully functional)

Authoring and presentation software:

Macromedia Director—Mac and Windows

Adobe Premiere—Mac and Windows

Imagebases:

DCI's ImageAXS—Mac and Windows

(Full working version included. Phone authorization required, call 800-449-6220)

Imaging drawing and processing software:

Adobe Photoshop—Mac and Windows

Adobe Illustrator—Mac only

Adobe After Effects—Mac only

DeBabelizer Lite and DeBabelizer Toolbox—Mac only

Macromedia FreeHand—Mac and Windows

Macromedia XRes—Mac only

Macromedia Extreme 3D—Mac only

Web authoring software:

Adobe PageMill—Mac only

Macromedia Shockwave—Mac only

Other:

Macromedia Sound Edit16—Mac & Windows

Macromedia Deck II—Mac only

Macromedia Fontographer Mac and Windows

Adobe Texture Maker Samples (12 backgrounds and buttons)—Mac and Windows

Adobe Streamline—Mac only

Adobe After Effects—Mac only

About the Contents of the CD-ROM

▶ All the images are 24-bit screen resolution (at least 640×480) and saved in the JPEG format. They can be opened and viewed on a Macintosh using the DCI ImageAXS software provided on the disc or on either a Mac or a PC by using any image processing program such as Photoshop. To import the images into programs such as Director, you will need to convert them into a compatible format. The author wishes to thank Scitex Corporation for their loan of a Scitex Smart 342L scanner, a highly sophisticated and versatile device, which was used to scan many of the images on the CD-ROM.

▶ The Corbis images are for personal use only. Any other use, including further reproduction or redistribution in any form or in any media (including online use) is strictly prohibited and could violate federal copyright law. If you wish to license other rights to these images or if you have other image content needs, contact Corbis directly at 800-260-0444. Be sure to request a free catalog that highlights the entire Corbis collection, and check out their Web site at www.corbis.com.

▶ The images by the author can be used royalty-free in digital productions. Resale in the form of clip media collections or as clip media is not permitted. For obtaining further rights (and other images) please contact the author at MikkelA@AOL.com.

▶ The DXM EARSHOT sample sound clips are saved as 16 bit/44.1kHz in the AIFF format. The complete two volume CD-ROM collection of 1,500 multimedia-ready sound effects is available for purchasers of this book at a special discount price of $109. To place an order, call 800-933-6223 or send an email to gmdesign1@aol.com. Be sure to mention *Still Images in Multimedia* to receive a discount. (Also be sure to check out DXM's website at: www.dxm.com.)

▶ You can view the Corbis or the author's imagery on a Macintosh with the ImageAXS imagebase included on the CD. This is a view-only version of the software and requires system 7.0 or greater. A full-working version is also included (version 1.5 for the Macintosh and version 2.5 for Windows) that you can purchase for $149. Simply copy the application to your system and call DCI at 800-449-6220. Once you have paid, they will give you an authorization code that will enable you to use the software.

▶ The limited edition of DeBabelizer Lite (Mac only) included on the CD-ROM is free to our readers and fully functional but only reads and writes PICT, BMP, TIFF, and GIF file formats. You can create slide shows from this version. The full-version, which is commonly sold for around $70, reads and writes over 40 file formats. A demo version of the top-of-the-line DeBabelizer Toolbox is also included on the CD-ROM. This program has all the features of DeBabelizer Lite but also includes image processing, palette manipulation, and internal scripting. It is commonly sold for around $270. (A Windows version of DeBabelizer will be available from Equilibrium later in 1996.) For further information contact the publisher directly at 415-332-4343 or at www.equilibrium.com.